T0049397

EVERYDAY FREEDOM

Designing the Framework
for a Flourishing Society

PHILIP K. HOWARD

RODIN
BOOKS™

RODIN BOOKS™

Hardcover ISBN 978-1-957588-20-9
eBook ISBN 978-1-957588-21-6

PUBLISHED BY RODIN BOOKS INC
666 Old Country Road
Suite 510
Garden City, New York 11530

www.rodinbooks.com

Book and cover design by Alexia Garaventa

Manufactured in the United States of America

To our grandchildren

Charlotte, Wyatt, Freddie, Alexandra, Ellie,
Alexander, Francesca, and Charlie

ALSO BY PHILIP K. HOWARD

The Death of Common Sense

The Collapse of the Common Good

Life Without Lawyers

The Rule of Nobody

Try Common Sense

Not Accountable

CONTENTS

Introduction   1

I.   The Human Need to Do Things Our Own Way   7

II.   Everyday Freedom Is Essential for Achievement   11

III.   Law after the 1960s: Replacing Institutional
Authority with Individual Rights   18

IV.   The Architecture of Everyday Freedom   24

V.   It's OK to Walk Away: The Flawed Assumptions
of Current Law that Cause Failure and Alienation   36

VI.   Rebuilding Trust for a Flourishing Society   53

VII.   Institutional Authority Is Vital to Everyday Freedom   67

VIII.   Community Responsibility and Social Cohesion   73

IX.   The Freedom to Save Ourselves   80

Notes   87

Acknowledgments   115

About the Author   119

INTRODUCTION

For twenty-five years, Ken Wagner had a front row seat to challenges in public schools, first as a teacher in New York and then as commissioner of education in Rhode Island. Wagner, now retired from public service, sums up school failures as a plague of powerlessness. In Rhode Island, he had to help pick up the pieces when the young and talented Providence school superintendent quit because he lacked authority to do the job—the sixth superintendent in Providence to leave in twenty years.

"The enemy is the system," Wagner concluded. "New teachers come into schools like candles. Then the system starts snuffing them out." Wagner gives a litany: Follow the lesson plan. Focus on standardized tests. No exceptions for that student. No, we can't fix the water leak. Prove in a legal hearing that the student was disruptive. Ignore the parents. Don't even think about being creative. Stay within the boundaries of the union contract. "After five or ten years, many teachers have had their spirit squeezed out of them. What's left are a few heroes in an impossible system."

Now compare Wagner's experience in schools with the diagnosis by Dr. Jesse Ehrenfeld, president of the American Medical Association, about the plague of physician burnout. Dr. Ehrenfeld describes "systemic issues in our healthcare system that have long been ignored: ever-growing administrative burdens that take us away from time with our patients; poorly functioning electronic health records . . . ; a pervasive sense of being powerless to fix the problems we encounter."

Now move over to careers within government. A sense of futility is the common complaint among public employees, as if they're swimming in a vast bureaucratic rip tide. Many public employees "learn they can't make a difference," a senior civil servant in Florida told me, "so they give up." This is one reason why recruiting new public employees is proving so difficult.

Now let's look at American culture. Something basic is missing. Americans know it. Nothing much works as it should. Simple daily choices seem fraught with peril. In the workplace, we walk on eggshells. Big projects—say, modernizing infrastructure—get stalled in years of review. Endemic social problems such as homelessness become, well, more endemic. Oh, there goes San Francisco. Doing what's right is not on the table. Who's to say what's right? Extremism grows.

Powerlessness has become a defining feature of modern society. Americans at all levels of responsibility feel powerless to do what they think is needed. The culture wars, sociologist James Davison Hunter explains, stem from institutional impotence: A "growing majority of Americans believe that their government cannot be trusted, that its leaders . . . are incompetent and self-interested, and that as citizens, they personally have little power to influence the . . . institutions or circumstances that shape their lives." Feeling fragile, and buffeted by forces beyond our control, many Americans retreat to online groups defined by identity and by distrust of the other side as "a threat to [our] existence."

It's hard to identify what's wrong amid the clamor and conflict in modern society. But a clue can be found in remembering what makes us proud. America is where people roll up our sleeves and get it done. The ability to do things in our own ways activates the values for which America is well-known: self-reliance, pragmatism, and loyalty to the greater good—what Alexis de Tocqueville called "self-interest, rightly understood." For most of American history, the power and imperative to own your actions and solutions—the concept of individual responsibility—was implicit in the idea of freedom.

Americans didn't abandon our belief in individual responsibility. It was taken away from us by a post 1960s legal framework that, with the best of intentions, made people squirm through the eye of a legal needle before taking responsibility.

Individual responsibility to a broader group, for example, was dislodged by a new concept of individual rights focused on what's best for one person or constituency. The can-do culture became the can't-do culture.

At every level of responsibility, Americans have lost the authority to do what they think is sensible. The teacher in the classroom, the principal in a school, the nurse in the hospital, the official in Washington, the parent on the field trip, the head of the local charity or church . . . all have their hands tied by real or feared legal constraints.

For several decades I've dissected the failures of government and discussed the need for simplified structures that allow government to accomplish its goals without stifling Americans' freedom. Leaders and intellectuals from both sides have embraced my diagnosis, but little has changed. America is apparently rich enough to endure continuing government ineptitude and waste.

I now see that the greater danger is not ineffective government, but the corrosion of American culture. Alienation has become a plague: Many Americans no longer believe in America. That's largely because, I argue here, they no longer have the freedom to take responsibility in their daily choices. Persistent failures feed the frustration and seed a culture of distrust. Instead of focusing on how to make things work, Americans obsess about what might go wrong.

The cure is not mainly new policies, but new legal operating structures that re-empower Americans in their everyday choices. People must have "everyday freedom," by which I mean the individual authority, at every level of society and every level of responsibility, to act as they feel appropriate, constrained only by the boundaries of law and by norms set by the employer or other institution. People must be free to draw on their skills, intuitions, and values when confronting daily challenges. They must own their actions. It is this ownership of choices that gives freedom its power and makes it the source of pride. That's how things get done sensibly and fairly.

In a crowded society, individual freedom also requires a framework for mutual trust. Here as well, everyday freedom is key to rebuilding a hierarchy of authority to protect against antisocial behavior. Restoring the authority to use judgment when applying law is as important for a judge and a public official as for a citizen. Indeed, I will argue that liberty in the broad sense requires judges and officials, when applying legal principles, to assert norms of reasonableness. Otherwise, self-interested people will use law to claim almost anything.

"Freedom" is used in many ways, often to support contradictory positions and policies. "Everyday freedom" is not directed at policy goals but is a philosophy of implementation and interaction. Letting people use their judgment when fulfilling responsibilities should be a goal of both progressives and conservatives. It's the only way to deliver good government. By empowering individuals to do what they think is sensible and right, it's also the only way to pull America out of the downward spiral of worsening failure, distrust, and alienation.

What should overhaul look like? I propose a new legal framework that replaces red tape and self-interested rights with individual responsibility and accountability. Instead of purging authority to prevent abuse, this framework rebuilds clear lines of authority to make common choices, to oversee those choices, and to define zones of protected freedom.

I.

THE HUMAN NEED TO DO THINGS OUR OWN WAY

Humans need agency. Waking up in the morning, most people want to make a difference in their jobs, families, or communities.

Liberty to pursue our own goals is how most people probably conceive of freedom. But that's only one aspect of freedom. People also need freedom in *how* we do things: "'Individual liberty is individual power,' the capacity to act to achieve one's ends," historian Eric Foner wrote in *The Story of American Freedom*, quoting John Quincy Adams. Making things happen is a powerful driver of individual energy and creativity. Pride and self-respect flow from our choices on how to carry out projects, on what we decide is fair and sensible, and on how we work with others to achieve things bigger than ourselves. Think of all the activities and accomplishments that you are proud of—whether in your career, your community, or your family. All happened in part because of your individual effort and ideas. Personal ownership of daily choices is the main way we express our commitment and character.

For most of human history, social struggles were aimed at big freedoms—replacing tyrants with democratic governance, and achieving equal rights for women and minorities. The freedom of people in daily activities was taken for granted. Printers, cobblers, and silversmiths, for example, had the pride of their craft. Farmers had the pride of hard work on land they knew. Healthy organizations, such as companies and universities, had an internal culture with definite norms that people could rely upon. Many communities throbbed with joint activities—such as running the school, providing social services, and organizing little leagues or holiday parades.

Starting in the 1960s, the social and legal institutions of America were remade to try to eliminate unfair choices by people in positions of responsibility. The new legal structures reflected a deep distrust of human authority in even its more benign forms—a teacher's authority in the classroom, or a manager's judgments about who's doing the job, or a university president's authority to enforce norms of civil discourse.

Individual responsibility was replaced by red tape and legal process. The goal was to enhance freedom by reducing any wiggle room for bias, unfairness, or error. The immediate effect was to remove the freedom to act on our best judgment. For example, teachers regurgitate mandatory lesson plans and are powerless to deal with disruptive students.

Another effect is a sense of repression, fueling the alienation against traditional institutions and social norms. Spontaneity in the workplace is suppressed, and free speech on campus is replaced by politically correct speech codes. Selfishness has filled the vacuum left by the loss of institutional authority, further eroding freedom. Centralized law and regulation aimed at compliance and conformity have hollowed out community institutions and discouraged local initiative. Deprived of opportunities to do things your way and to join with others to make a difference, many people withdraw into pockets of resistance and lay blame on "the other." The land of opportunity has become the land of distrust.

Suppressing daily freedoms causes many people to give up. Tocqueville feared that democracy, in a quest for equality, might mandate conformity in daily life. Extending state control to daily decisions, he thought, would kill the American spirit:

> It is especially dangerous to enslave men in the minor details of life. For my own part, I should be inclined to think freedom less necessary in great things than in little ones . . . Subjection in minor affairs . . . does not drive men to resistance, but it crosses them at every turn, till they are led to surrender the exercise of their own will. Thus their spirit is gradually broken and their character enervated.

Modern law didn't mean to suffocate the human spirit. It just meant to preclude unfairness. But, as I discuss now, people can't be programmed like a computer. Most decisions are not even the result of conscious reasoning. Human intelligence resides largely in the unconscious part of the brain. Most achievement requires adaptation on the spot. Nor can social relations be programmed. Human perception can be repressed but not cancelled. We see what we see.

II.

EVERYDAY FREEDOM IS ESSENTIAL FOR ACHIEVEMENT

Human choice on the spot is indispensable to the success of most activities. Achievement generally hinges in large part on the judgment, skill, energy, and values of the people involved—the mother, the doctor, the repairman, the foreman, and others. Management theorist Chester Barnard thought that "nine-tenths of all organization activity is on the responsibility, the authority . . . of those who make the last contributions, who apply personal energies to the final concrete objectives."

Organizational tools and protocols only take us so far. People must apply themselves to finish the job. Even repetitious activities, such as assembly lines, require human oversight and adjustment. The power of artificial intelligence is an advancing frontier, with limits yet to be discovered. AI tools are likely to significantly enhance the power and productivity of individuals, but many experts believe that AI cannot be left alone. AI is a black box, without reliable constraints of social norms and without empathy.

Everyday freedom is also relevant to social policy because it enables officials as well as citizens to do what's needed to meet public goals. Teachers in the classroom, cops on the beat, supervisors in the workplace, inspectors for public agencies, work crews on the roads, officials in charge of public permits . . . all need the freedom to make sense of the situations confronting them. Most failures of government cannot fairly be pinned on excessive regulatory goals. They're failures of execution—lousy schools, unaccountable cops, decade-long permitting, inefficient and unresponsive public services—that, as I will discuss, stem directly or indirectly from the powerlessness of public employees on the ground.

Partisans on both sides argue about policy goals, but neither side presents a vision of how better to run the operations of government. What's lost in our time are the microeconomic truths of how humans and institutions achieve things. Daily achievements of most people consist of many small and large choices. The freedom to make these daily choices is the essential mechanism by which anything good happens.

Everyday freedom unleashes human capabilities in two vital ways. First, as noted, everyday freedom liberates people to take ownership for how things happen. These choices invariably involve uncertainty, risk of failure and, often, moral judgments about right and wrong. Personal ownership of those choices is what energizes people and engages their creativity. The freedom to interact spontaneously with others is also a condition of healthy relationships and mutual trust, and, Hannah Arendt thought, is the "most elementary manifestation of human freedom."

Everyday freedom is also indispensable because not much gets done, at least not sensibly, unless people can act on their perceptions, intuitions, and values. This is for cognitive reasons: People lack the capacity to rely on reason or logic to adapt, innovate, or interact effectively. The elements of effective action predominantly come from the unconscious part of the brain, not the conscious part. Our perception and intuitions, developed by training and experience, are melded together in that deep unconscious and emerge as action or a presumption of what to do.

In repetitious tasks, action flows spontaneously from the unconscious, barely waving at our conscious brain as it emerges from a person as speech or decisions. In *The Mind at Work*, Mike Rose describes how waiters, carpenters, plumbers, and others "disappear . . . into the task." Their judgment is reflected in their actions, not conscious thought: Our knowledge is in our action.

Sully Sullenberger, the pilot of the airliner that lost its power shortly after takeoff in New York, drew on his instincts to maintain a downward trajectory sufficient to maintain airspeed long enough to safely ditch the plane in the Hudson River. As William Langewiesche described in *Fly by Wire*, Sullenberger "did not sit in airplanes so much as put them on. He flew them in a profoundly integrated way, as an expression of himself." Sullenberger's own recollection of the last seconds before hitting the river reveal the power of intuition: "The earth and the river were rushing toward us . . . At that instant, I judged it was the right time . . . I pulled the side stick back, farther back, finally full aft, and held it there as we touched the water."

Self-consciousness—making people think through their actions—will often cause failure when people are accessing muscle memory or reacting to immediate situations. A pianist cannot play the piece, chemist and philosopher Michael Polanyi observes in *Personal Knowledge*, if she thinks about how she is hitting the notes. For activities that involve sensory or personal taste, studies suggest that people make worse judgments when they know they must justify them.

In his essay "The Emotional Dog and Its Rational Tail," social psychologist Jonathan Haidt explains how moral choices, and decisions about right conduct, also emerge almost spontaneously from the unconscious.

But human decision-making is flawed in predictable ways, as Daniel Kahneman and others have shown; for example, people tend to avoid potential losses more than they value potential gains. There is an enormous body of psychological study about the relative strengths of intuitive choices (known as "system 1") and reflective reasoning ("system 2").

Pausing and getting input is wise for many strategic decisions, such as feedback from colleagues, friends, or from the public. Surveys and trials can provide valuable input before committing resources. A second approval, or rule-of-thumb protocols, can be useful to avoid mistakes. A rote checklist is vital in situations where a small error can result in disaster, such as a pilot forgetting to push a button before a plane takes off, or a surgeon operating on the wrong limb. Having gone through the checklist, however, the surgeon "disappears into the task" largely guided by perception and experience.

It is often said about effective people that they have "good judgment," implying that they reason their way towards successful outcomes. But that's a "rationalist delusion," Jonathan Haidt explains. Even where people are reflecting on what to do, the ultimate choice is usually an intuition that the person can't break down into parts. Michael Polanyi describes how people engage in the "usual process of unconscious trial and error by which we *feel our way* to success . . . without specifically knowing how we do it." In his essay "The Dog and the Frisbee," Andrew Haldane, former chief economist for The Bank of England, compares the instinctual foundation of monetary policy with the skill of a dog to catch frisbees. Scientific discovery, Polanyi believed, involves a kind of dialectic between intuitive and analytical skills, but "intuitive powers . . . are dominant and decisive."

Only the final confirmation of a scientific discovery is a matter of objective proof.

Conscious deliberation can act as a kind of filter to avoid rash decisions or to add inputs that inform decisions, although more often, Haidt explains, reasoning is used to rationalize intuitions. Even with deliberation and analysis, final judgments are still largely intuitive. Management theorist Peter Drucker observed that "amazingly few people know how they get things done."

Freedom doesn't guarantee success, of course. Failure is the main learning tool of progress—the process of trial and error. Consistently poor decisions or performance is one reason why accountability is critical. Each of us is better at some things than at others. Taking responsibility also reveals our sense of morality. Everyday freedom operates in a kind of marketplace in which people are free to make judgments about other people, and to decide whether they want to deal with you, or buy your products or services.

People judging people is the currency of social interaction, and cannot be expunged even if we wanted to. Like atoms in a test tube, people in a free society bounce here and there and form alliances with others. Teachers who don't succeed in one school can thrive in another.

The unconscious aspects of human decision-making also incorporate unconscious biases. Law has a role to play in pushing against these biases, for example, by banning discriminatory practices. Studies show that trying too hard to purge bias, on the other hand, has the paradoxical effect of reaffirming or causing bias. Successful relationships require candor and mutual respect, not a muzzle.

"It's not rocket science," former Rhode Island Education Commissioner Ken Wagner observed about good schools: "Give everyone a sense of ownership, including students. Principals and teachers should have the freedom to do what's needed to engage students—including, especially, drawing on their personalities and passions. What's effective, generally, is what students think is interesting. Visit a school, and you can tell in five minutes whether teachers and students feel part of a learning culture."

No legal framework can supplant the human perceptions and instincts needed to get things done. The power of daily choices by each individual is probably the most important resource of a free society. That belief in individual and institutional initiative—the power and pride of American culture—was smothered by the legal structure erected starting in the 1960s.

III.

LAW AFTER THE 1960S: REPLACING INSTITUTIONAL AUTHORITY WITH INDIVIDUAL RIGHTS

The tumultuous decade of the 1960s was a reaction to serial abuses of authority, including segregation, pollution, gender discrimination, unsafe cars, Vietnam, and, in the early 1970s, Watergate. Changing law to reflect better social values was essential. But how could society protect against future abuses?

Freedom was reconceived as a concept of individual rights against anyone with authority. Instead of a concept of human agency, including for people with responsibility, there was "a massive redefinition of freedom," historian Eric Foner found, "as a rejection of all authority."

The 1960s "rights revolution" transformed institutional choices. Government was the first domino to fall. Any public decision, including personnel choices, school discipline, and public contracts and permits, was not valid unless officials could demonstrate why their decision did not abuse their authority. Government decisions, law professor Charles Reich argued, should be considered the "new property" of each individual. Focusing on individual rights, he argued, was necessary because legislatures often have a "simplistic notion of public interest" that undermines "the independence of the individual."

If a public employee had rights against abuse of authority, why not private employees? The civil rights movement focused on protections against racial discrimination. Why not against discrimination of any sort? Any adverse personnel decision became legally suspect. Reich approved: It is "not any particular power, but all kinds of power, that are to be feared."

After the 1960s, the framework of American law was largely rebuilt, with three new legal mechanisms aimed at safeguarding against decisions by people with authority:

1. *Prescriptive rulebooks*, wherever possible, would dictate "one correct way" to do things. For forest rangers in national parks, volumes of detailed rules replaced the pamphlet that used to guide their activities. Safety in the workplace was regulated not by unsafe practices but by thousands of rules— many self-evident, trivial, or overbearing, such as requirements to illuminate stairwells, maintain neat closets, and use industrial grade hammers. Before the 1960s, there was no such thing as thousand-page rulebooks. But at the turn of the

twentieth century, theorists such as Max Weber
and Frederick Winslow Taylor thought that rigorous systems could dictate a "fixed route of march"
without the need for human judgment, thereby
avoiding the risk of human fallibility. Experts
after the 1960s grabbed onto these theories like a
life preserver: "Only precise, specific guidelines,"
Brookings scholar Herbert Kaufman wrote, "can
assure common treatment of like cases."

2. For decisions that cannot be dictated in advance,
formal procedures would force officials to provide
proof of the correctness of their decisions. Proof
of objective facts, the theory went, would resolve
any dispute. The "legal process" movement was
the brainchild of law professors Henry Hart and
Albert Sachs, who argued that law should not
provide "final answers" but should be "content
neutral," and provide "an agreeable procedure for
getting acceptable answers." These procedures
soon took a life of their own. Giving a permit to
modernize infrastructure, or disciplining a public
employee, began to take years.

3. The *new litmus test of individual rights* empowered
people to file a lawsuit for any adverse life event
and to throw a legal monkey wrench into any
decisions they disagreed with. Instead of being a
protection against state power, these new rights
let people invoke state power to address personal

disappointments in the workplace or in schools. Almost any ordinary accident, say a fall on a playground, could be dressed up as an outrage with the benefit of hindsight. Why wasn't there better supervision of the kids at the swing set? But these rights had a common theme: they seemed to be selfishness dressed up in legal clothes—"conclusions masquerading as reasons," in the words of legal scholar Cass Sunstein.

Because the new legal framework embodied new values, including protections against racism, pollution, and unsafe cars, it enjoys a halo of virtue. But pulling down the hierarchy of authority was not the only or the best way to achieve those new values. I will shortly describe why these new legal mechanisms caused the collapse of the framework of freedom.

The collateral damage to American culture and to daily freedoms is there for all to see. One casualty is the common good. Looking for violations of rights through a legal magnifying glass changed the goals of society: Instead of governing for the common good, the first value has become avoiding any possible violation of individual rights. Rights carry the connotation of being absolute, a kind of legal trump card, that doesn't leave open the possibility of compromise or trade-offs. While Justice Oliver Wendell Holmes, Jr., said that law should weigh "considerations of social advantage," philosopher John Rawls in 1971 embraced the idea that rights are not "subject to . . . the calculus of social interests."

America started governing for the lowest common denominator: You can't build the transmission line to access renewable power because one group doesn't want it; you can't terminate a bad cop because you might terminate a good cop; you must cancel the nature field trip because one disabled student can't go.

Everyday decisions became pregnant with legal ramifications. Instead of relieving citizens of anxiety, law created new legal anxieties and risks. The original big idea of protecting against state coercion seeped down into practically every societal interaction. Employers stopped giving honest performance reviews or job references. Doctors avoided candor with colleagues and practiced defensive medicine. Schools restricted children's play. Vital institutions diverted huge parts of their budgets to legal compliance. Police departments, schools, and other public departments became less effective because the people in charge no longer had management authority. Public institutions lost their ability to move forward, as if their hub was disconnected from the spokes.

Society without authority was cast adrift, gradually losing sight of values that people could trust in social dealings. Political scientist Alan Wolfe found that Americans had "lost the distinction between right and wrong and desperately want it back." A free society requires a framework of norms that people can rely upon, not rejection of legal norms as "a form of authoritarianism."

Sociologist Nathan Glazer was there at the creation. The 1960s were "a new age in which we would rationally and pragmatically attack our domestic social problems. We could relegate the ideological conflicts . . . to the past because we now knew more and . . . had the tools . . . to do better." The smartest people in America were in Washington inventing a new social order. But the new system seemed to be causing conflict, not solving it. "By the end of the 1960s," Glazer observed, "I was not alone in thinking that something had gone wrong . . . We seemed to be creating as many problems as we were solving."

Post–1960s law put tight legal controls on daily choices to prevent people with responsibility from making bad choices. It aims to create a utopia of interlocking rights—a kind of "crossword puzzle to be solved . . . one correct way," as Václav Havel put it. But freedom is supposed to empower people to do things in many different ways. Conflicting interests are unavoidable and cannot be avoided by looking at every dispute as a matter of rights. Law must assert norms of right and wrong. This requires an entirely different legal framework. Instead of "the increasing delegitimization of authority," as I discuss now, a framework for everyday freedom requires the active assertion of social norms by people in authority.

IV.

THE ARCHITECTURE OF EVERYDAY FREEDOM

How a legal framework operates to protect everyday freedom is largely agnostic as to policy. It requires assertion of norms, but mainly in application, not to create new policy norms. Applying existing norms to defend the scope of reasonable freedom is the job of judges and officials.

Generally, the rule of law aims to support freedom by reducing distrust in social dealings. Criminals will be put in jail. People who break contracts will be held to account. Regulation protects against adulterated food and other unsafe products. Trust that law will protect against abuses liberates people to focus on their goals, not on self-protection.

Whether a legal framework is effective in supporting a free society is judged not by what it prohibits, but by the scope of what people feel empowered to do. "The end of law is not to . . . restrain," John Locke noted, "but to preserve and enlarge freedom." Law is effective if we feel free to walk on crowded streets, interact spontaneously in our daily dealings, and take initiative. The extent of your freedom is roughly correlated with the level of your trust in law.

Modern law is overinclusive at trying to block abuses and fails badly when evaluated as the protector of reasonable freedoms. On a daily basis, Americans don't feel free to do what's right. Citizens find themselves stymied by complex legal dictates and by legal risk. Elected and appointed officials no longer have authority to fire a rogue cop or to overhaul failing schools.

Modern law lost the memo about supporting freedom. Instead of a framework for human freedom, it's an elaborate precautionary system aimed at precluding human error. Anything that goes wrong, any accident or disappointment, any disagreement, potentially requires a legal solution. Instead of charging officials to do what's sensible, modern law presumes that the gravest risk is to leave room for the judgment of people in positions of authority. Who knows what evil might be done by a school principal, or environmental official, or supervisor?

Instead of nurturing social trust, law after the 1960s infected society with distrust. Indeed, as I will discuss, law has elevated distrust into a social obsession. Yes, of course people are fallible, but an arbitrary decision can be overturned. An abuse of power should get the person fired. There is no Attila the Hun lurking in the closet, ready to brutalize society as soon as the door to human judgment is unlocked.

Letting people with responsibility use their judgment is what democracy requires, not a risk to be avoided. As James Madison put it:

> It is one of the most prominent features of the constitution, a principle that pervades the whole system, that there should be the highest possible degree of responsibility in all the Executive officers thereof; anything, therefor, which tends to lessen this responsibility is contrary to its spirit and intention.

Justice too requires applying judgment to the facts in each situation. "Justice is a concept by far more subtle and indefinite than is yielded by mere obedience to a rule," Benjamin Cardozo noted. Moral philosophers since Aristotle have made the same point: "The task of making a moral decision is that of doing the right thing in a particular situation," Hans-Georg Gadamer observed: "Moral knowledge can never be knowable in advance."

To the modern mind, it seems like anarchy to let judges and public officials make decisions in context. But they are not deciding in a vacuum—they are bound to follow principles, as I will shortly discuss, and will be accountable if they do otherwise. How else can law match our ethical sensibilities? The letter of the law is too detailed, too cold and formal, too readily gamed for self-interest. Law's effectiveness ultimately hinges on trust by America's three-hundred-million-odd

citizens that law will support their reasonable under-
standings of right and wrong.

The framework of law that supports everyday
freedom has a specific architecture. Instead of a dense
thicket of rules and processes, enforced by inquisi-
tions into possible error and imperfection, law should
consist of outer boundaries that protect against abuse
while defining and preserving a broad area of freedom
in which law will not intercede.

This legal structure has three key parts:

1. Law should define boundaries safeguarding
   against unreasonable acts and enclosing an open
   field of freedom on which people can interact
   without fear of abuse or legal ramifications;

2. The legal boundaries should be defined mainly
   using broad principles, not detailed rules;

3. Law should restore clear lines of authority to
   interpret and enforce these legal principles. When
   norms are in flux, someone in authority must draw
   the line.

A rule of law built with these components could
hardly be more traditional. The effect on people's
daily choices could hardly be more positive. Instead
of fighting through a legal jungle fraught with claims
and fears, Americans can make daily decisions based
on reasonable social norms: What's the right thing to
do here?

First legal element for everyday freedom: **Law should set outer boundaries against impermissible conduct, not dictate correct choices.**

Law is supposed to be a framework of outer boundaries, not an instruction manual for life choices. Think of law as a fence creating a giant corral defining a field of freedom. Law should set "frontiers, not artificially drawn," as Isaiah Berlin observed, "within which men should be inviolable." The legal fence has two roles: On the outside of the fence, law protects against acts that are not allowed, such as violence, theft, breach of contract, or sale of defective products—protecting our "freedom from" coercion and abuse.

On the inside, law defines a field of freedom in which people are free to interact as they wish. This role of law preserves our "freedom to" do things our own way—our "unalienable rights" of "life, liberty, and the pursuit of happiness" that cannot be taken away, even by government.

The liberating role of the rule of law—preserving an open field of free interaction—unleashes resourcefulness, trial and error, and managerial instincts essential to achieving success in competitive markets. This liberating role empowers humans to flourish in many non-economic ways—to live by their own values, and to affiliate with others who are like-minded, to volunteer in a community, and to be creative and to take risks in pursuit of personal goals. In these and other ways, the rule of law dramatically expands economic and social productivity.

Law as a framework of boundaries is a forgotten idea. Instead of safeguarding an open field of freedom, as I will discuss, law has created a legal minefield.

Second legal element for everyday freedom: **Legal boundaries should be made of broad principles, not precise rules.**

Legal boundaries should consist mainly of legal principles, not dictates for how to make daily choices. Law based on legal principles has significant advantages over detailed law. Because principles are activated by human judgment on the spot, principles let people adapt to particular circumstances. Instead of mindless compliance with preset dictates, principles-based law is built on the bedrock of human responsibility. Principles honor human agency.

The U.S. Constitution mainly consists of principles. Article II vests the president with "executive Power" without defining exactly what that means. The First Amendment provides for freedom of speech, the Fourth Amendment prohibits "unreasonable searches and seizures" and the Fifth Amendment provides that no person shall be "deprived of life, liberty, or property, without due process of law." All these pillars of freedom are not defined further, but are interpreted by numerous judicial decisions, and have proved effective as bulwarks against state coercion.

Principles-based law authorizes people to take into account immediate circumstances. Under the Fourth Amendment, for example, a police officer can break into a home to protect a person from imminent danger, but an officer needs a search warrant to enter a home to try to find evidence of a crime. By tethering law to social norms of what's reasonable, principles-based law achieves what Oliver Wendell Holmes, Jr., thought was "the first requirement of a sound body of law": that "it should correspond to the actual feelings and demands of the community."

Principles are far superior to detailed rules for regulating most activities. Principles let people focus on achieving goals, not checking boxes. People can adapt as situations change. In the 1980s, Australia replaced its prescriptive regulatory requirements for nursing homes with thirty-one general principles—for example, to provide a "homelike environment." Within a short period, nursing homes markedly improved. The major difference was that everyone involved—nursing home operators, nurse aides, family members, and regulators—could now focus on making the nursing home better. Nursing homes were also free to innovate, such as with gardens and other amenities that residents sought.

By contrast, specific instructions on how to do things properly is generally a formula for failure. Detailed rules, striving for completeness, cause failure not only by preempting human judgment, but also by diverting human focus, wasting time, and skewing priorities towards compliance with secondary or trivial goals. Is your paperwork in order? An irony of so-called "clear rules" is that they are too detailed to be knowable even by inspectors whose job it is to enforce them.

Principles, unlike prescriptive rules, don't aspire to literal certainty. What principles offer instead is coherence—principles such as "unreasonable searches and seizures" or a "homelike environment" are readily internalized. As Judge Richard Posner observed, "standards that capture lay intuitions about right behavior may produce greater legal certainty than a network of precise but technical non-intuitive rules."

A measure of uncertainty empowers every stakeholder. In Australia, nursing home personnel could draw on their perceptions and instincts to do what they thought made sense. Residents and family members could draw on their perceptions to suggest improvements. Inspectors could draw on their experience to require improvements. If a nursing home operator disagreed, he could challenge the inspector's order up the chain of agency authority, and ultimately to a court. All stakeholders were at risk for the reasonableness of their positions.

People are "mightily addicted to rules," Hume observed. Just tell us what's required. But life is too complicated to be lived out of a rulebook. The gray areas at the boundaries of principles-based law tend to keep people honest. Uncertainty all around is a powerful driver for people to negotiate and reach an accommodation. By contrast, prescriptive rules drive people to parse legal language and make legalistic arguments that are disconnected from problem-solving. You think you're in compliance with regulations? Let me check. You say I have to teach during a pandemic? The union contract says nothing about distance learning. Precise rules that strive "to cover every case," philosopher John Dewey observed, encourage "shrewd and enterprising men . . . to sail close to the wind, and to trust to ingenious lawyers to . . . go scot free."

The uncertainty inherent in principles-based law drives most people to act in the middle lane of accepted norms. The safeguard against arbitrary or inappropriate decisions is not rote compliance but the oversight by other people—coworkers, supervisors, family members, regulators, and ultimately courts. Principles put a ring around the scope of allowable authority, "like the hole in a doughnut," in the word of legal philosopher Ronald Dworkin: An official's flexibility "means not that he is free to decide without recourse to standards of sense and fairness."

The Role of Precise Rules

Some areas of regulation are not conducive to principles. It would be hard to regulate pollution by a reasonableness standard, for example. In "The Optimum Precision of Administrative Rules," Professor Colin Diver applied a utilitarian test to decide where specific rules—say, the seatbelt mandate, or maximum age cutoff for commercial pilots—are preferable to principles-based frameworks.

There are also situations that call for detailed checklists, where the disastrous effects of one small mistake put a premium on rigorous protocols. Management professor Brenda Zimmerman drew the distinction between "complicated" and "complex" activities. In "complicated" activities—say, a space launch with many moving parts—it's vital to make sure no detail has been overlooked. But in what Professor Zimmerman called "complex" activities—for example, presiding over a classroom of thirty students, or managing multiple resources in any institution—rigid rules and checklists can be counterproductive. Those activities require trade-offs, and trial and error, and perceptions of how best to balance competing demands.

Many activities require a hybrid approach. Safety in the workplace, for example, is mainly a function of training and work culture, where principles are preferable. But there are also protocols, such as wearing a hard hat, that should be a rule.

A principles-based legal framework is superior in almost all respects to the tangle of modern law. Principles are understandable, keep people focused on legal goals, and leave ample room for people to achieve those goals. Americans can act like Americans again. Whatever works is good.

Third legal element for everyday freedom: **Restore the interpretive authority of judges and public officials.**

The designated villain of post–1960s law is authority. But

America needed new values, not a legal system purged of decision-making authority. Freedom degenerates into a free-for-all if judges and officials lack the authority to defend the boundaries of prevailing social norms.

Authority conjures up nightmares of a society-wide drill instructor. But the way authority works in law, and the way it works for daily choices in most healthy organizations, is more like a security guard at the door, protecting against misconduct, not telling people how to do things. Authority at the legal boundaries is generally cautionary, not prescriptive. The citizen is free to do what he likes, and is at risk of legal consequences only when he strays over legal boundaries as defined and enforced ultimately by courts.

Management authority is indispensable for any functioning organization, especially government. There is a concentric quality to freedom in social organizations. Your freedom to use common sense is dependent upon supervisors and officials having the freedom to use their common sense:

- If teachers don't have authority to maintain order, the resulting disruption will deprive students of their freedom to learn.

- If supervisors lack authority to enforce standards of excellence, employees will soon find themselves shackled to bureaucratic rules dictating how to do their work, and condemned to a lackluster work culture without energy or pride.

- If inspectors lack authority to focus on the goals of regulation, the business will soon find itself with multiple violations of technical requirements that matter to no one.

- If hospital administrators must comply with dense bureaucratic and reimbursement rules, doctors and nurses will waste half their days in desk work and suffer burnout.

- If university presidents and deans don't enforce norms of civil discourse, professors and students lose their freedom to say what they really think.

Modern law tried to create a government better than people. No authority needed. But a system of rules without authority is central planning. Process without authority is paralysis. Self-defined rights against other citizens is tyranny. Authority in a democracy is merely another word for the freedom needed by officials to fulfill their responsibilities, subject always to review by other officials and judges. Take away the authority of people with responsibility, and a flourishing culture is soon replaced by futility and alienation.

V.

IT'S OK TO WALK AWAY: THE FLAWED ASSUMPTIONS OF CURRENT LAW THAT CAUSE FAILURE AND ALIENATION

Sooner or later, historians will view America's post–1960s legal framework as an experiment that failed. For us today, the challenge is to mobilize an intervention to break free of the addiction to this hands-free legal system. Americans must understand that the disease consuming the American spirit is caused by a legal framework aimed at human disempowerment.

Each of the core mechanisms of this legal framework—precise dictates, objective proof in legal proceedings, and satisfying individual rights as a litmus test—is taught in law schools as a virtuous hallmark of fair law. In the real world, each one undermines the everyday freedom essential for a healthy, functioning society.

Because inertia is such a powerful force it's critical to understand how these core precepts supplant human responsibility. I've analyzed the flaws of this anti-human system extensively in prior writings, looked at the evidence for three decades, and see no possibility of tweaking the system to make it work.

"When you strike at a king," Emerson observed, "you must kill him." Here are the reasons why the structure built since the 1960s must be abandoned, not amended, and, area by area, replaced by a framework activated by human responsibility.

How the Quest for "Clear Law" Guarantees Failure and Frustration

The experts in the 1960s thought that "clear law" could provide a template for daily choices—like, say, a software program. Government officials in white lab coats would simply follow the rules.

To be fair, many smart people embraced this rote compliance vision of government. Friedrich Hayek, in his 1944 book *The Road to Serfdom*, famously declared: "Government in all its actions [should be] bound by rules fixed and announced beforehand." This rationalistic vision of government was also a dream of the Enlightenment. "Let all the laws be clear, uniform, and precise," Voltaire believed: "To interpret laws is almost always to corrupt them."

But "clear law" is generally a myth. Most of what government does is far too complicated to "go by the book": Regulating safe products, permitting infrastructure, enforcing trade agreements, overseeing social facilities, procuring government contracts, not to mention running a school or police department, or presiding over a courtroom, all require officials and judges to exercise judgment.

"Clear law" also fails to acknowledge the unavoidable ambiguities in language, muddled further by the unforeseeable complexities of real life. As legal philosopher Jeremy Waldron put it: "Words do not determine meaning, people do. No amount of staring at the words of a rule, then staring at the world, then staring at the words again, will tell us when we have a proper application." Legal dictates not infrequently are contradictory, without any mechanism to make trade-offs. Permits for modernizing infrastructure get stalled by the need to choose between, say, clean energy or pristine vistas, or between preserving natural habitats or relieving traffic bottlenecks.

What's fair generally depends upon the circumstances. Because "the world, like a kaleidoscope, never exactly repeats any prior situation," Michael Polanyi explained, "we can achieve consistency only by identifying manifestly different situations in respect to some particular feature, and this requires a series of personal judgments." In most social situations, taking away human judgment usually guarantees unfairness: "A result arrived at by applying strict rules mechanically," Polanyi notes, "can mean nothing to anybody." Zero-tolerance rules in schools, for example, practically guarantee unfairness. Bringing a toy soldier carrying a tiny replica gun to school is different from bringing an actual gun. A first-grader giving unwanted kisses to a classmate should be treated differently from a twelfth-grader. A student misbehaving after the death of a family member should be given some slack.

The compulsive drive to write "clear law" has evolved into a manic disorder of modern democracy. For federal regulation alone, there are about 150 million words of binding legal requirements. No one can know it all, much less comply with it. Because the legal detail cannot be internalized, people suffer from "cognitive overload" trying to manage it in the conscious part of the brain, contributing to exhaustion, burnout, and failure. In their study of Illinois nursing home regulation, John and Valerie Braithwaite found that inspectors couldn't keep it all straight and typically enforced only about 10 percent of the rules. But which 10 percent varied by inspector.

Unknowable law, enforced arbitrarily, no longer has the quality of law. James Madison noted, "It will be of little avail to the people, that the laws are made by men of their own choice, if the laws be so voluminous that they cannot be read, or so incoherent that they cannot be understood." The quest for clear law has led America deep into a legal jungle, with no line of sight to do what's sensible and right.

Modern Process Precludes Human Responsibility

Not every decision can have a rule. Someone must

decide whether to give a permit for a new transmission line, say, or to remove an unruly student from the classroom. To guard against unfairness, these choices can often be reviewed by other people with knowledge of the situation. But post–1960s law, as noted, has a different concept: Make the responsible person prove the correctness of the decision in a formal process.

As a *tool for informing judgment*, process can be helpful. To instill trust in personnel decisions, for example, most large employers have a review process before terminating an employee. Environmental reviews, when focused on significant impacts, can provide transparency and public input before an infrastructure project is approved.

As a *mechanism to prove judgment*, however, procedures deter responsible choices and cause paralysis. Personnel choices, for example, are not susceptible to objective verification. How do you prove someone doesn't try hard, or is uncooperative, or has bad judgment? Or how do you prove that a teacher just goes through the motions, or doesn't engage students? In *The Moral Life of Schools*, Professor Philip Jackson and colleagues found that whether teachers were effective or ineffective often turned on subtle personality traits. Here is what the head of a charter school told me about why the school terminated a teacher who, on paper, should have been perfect:

> We had a teacher here—a really nice guy with
> great credentials and several years of teaching

under his belt—who just couldn't relate to the students. It's hard to put my fingers on exactly why. He would blow a little hot and cold, letting one student get away with talking in class and then coming down hard on someone else who did the same thing . . . But the effect was that kids started arguing back. It affected the whole school. Kids would come out of his class in a belligerent mood . . . We worked with him on classroom management the summer after his first year. It usually helps, but he just didn't have the knack. So we had to let him go.

Making people prove judgments that are based on perceptions and intuitions removes the everyday freedom needed to make things work. The proof is in the pudding. In each of the following areas, process as a substitute for human authority causes failure:

- *Process designed to protect the environment can harm the environment.* Instead of focusing on material impacts, environmental reviews are an exercise in trivial impacts—a process of no pebble left unturned. Sometimes thousands of pages long, environmental impact statements obscure rather than illuminate key trade-offs. In my report, "Two Years, Not Ten Years," I found that the delays harm the environment by prolonging bottlenecks and more than double the cost of most projects. Building new transmission lines to connect renewable energy sources has proved nearly impossible because of procedural hurdles in multiple jurisdictions.

- *Public supervisors no longer make supervisory judgments.* There's near-zero accountability for performance at every level of American government. Over an eighteen-year study period in Illinois, an average of two teachers out of ninety-five thousand were dismissed for poor performance—about .002 percent. Over 99 percent of federal employees are rated "fully successful." The lack of accountability not only keeps poor performers in place, but also corrodes the basis for mutual trust needed for a healthy institutional culture. As I describe in *Not Accountable*, the absence of accountability means that voters elect governors and mayors who lack authority to manage public operations.

- *Process designed to avoid injustice can cause injustice.* Because teachers and school administrators don't have time to prepare for and attend hearings on student discipline, they tolerate disorder. This in turn fosters more disorder, making learning within a classroom practically impossible. As sociologist Richard Arum found in *Judging School Discipline*, "it is this hesitation, doubt, and weakening of conviction . . . that has undermined the effectiveness of school discipline."

Because procedures designed to assure a fair trial in criminal cases now require multiple hearings over several years, Professor William Stuntz found in *The Collapse of American Criminal Justice*, many defendants can no longer afford to go to trial. It's too expensive to pay lawyers for all those hearings, so defendants are encouraged to plea bargain even if they are innocent. Companies will pay billions to settle mass tort actions, even where the science shows no link to their product; as one CEO put it, "we can't afford to keep winning cases." Too much process also undermines law enforcement. Requiring cops to demonstrate probable cause by objective facts has bred the cynical practice of "testilying"—when police make up some fact that will justify the stop. As psychologist Gerd Gigerenzer observes, the "insistence on after-the-fact justification ignores that good expert judgment is generally of an intuitive nature."

Almost no one actually succeeds in trekking to the end of the legal process rainbow. Instead of guaranteeing trustworthy public choices, extensive process has spawned a kind of black market in which citizens buy their way out of the endless legal ordeal—by paying off opposition groups to get a permit, or agreeing to a plea bargain with the prosecutor, or giving rich fees to class action lawyers, or promoting an unwanted teacher to an administrative position where he can do less harm.

The safeguard against arbitrary or unfair choices should be oversight by others, not an illusory quest for objective proof. "Objectivism has totally falsified our conception of truth," Polanyi concluded, "by exalting what we can know and prove, while covering up . . . all that we know and cannot prove."

Individual Rights Are Not Supposed to Be a Sword against Others' Freedom

Individual rights are supposed to be a shield, not a sword. The rights in the Constitution protect our freedom against state coercion. Due process, for example, protects against the state taking our property or throwing us in jail without "due process of law." The First Amendment protects freedom of speech. Because of distrust of royal judges, the Sixth Amendment guarantees that a jury must decide criminal convictions and the Seventh Amendment provides that a jury must resolve disputed facts in civil cases. In these and other ways, the Constitution shields our freedom against abuses of state power.

After the 1960s, however, the shield of individual rights was transformed into a sword against decisions by other free individuals, particularly those with responsibility. Rights against what? Decisions by people with responsibility. Authority of almost every kind, including management of a school or business, was put in the penalty box. Personnel decisions became fraught with legal risk. Civil rights laws aimed at ending systemic racial discrimination were expanded to challenge individual disappointments—not just based on race but any one of many "protected categories," and often against employers with exemplary records of inclusion.

Claiming individual rights became a weapon for selfishness. This new concept of rights naturally migrated to most areas of social interaction. A Public Agenda survey found that 78 percent of teachers had been accused by students of violating their rights. College students regularly assert that certain books, or words, or political positions, make them feel "unsafe," and therefore violate their rights.

The field of freedom, now overgrown with a thicket of red tape, was invaded by self-appointed rights-bearers demanding tribute. Extremists on the left asserted rights as an entitlement owed because of historical injustice, a guaranty against unequal outcomes, and protection from different points of view. Extremists on the right asserted rights against control of assault weapons, against COVID-19 public health decisions, and against books they disapprove of.

These new rights smashed what was left of everyday freedom. Instead of creating conditions for trust in social interaction, law became the source of distrust. In the land of the First Amendment, employers don't provide candid feedback, and college professors and students no longer feel free to say what they believe. Government became largely unmanageable under the elaborate rights demanded by public employee unions.

Repairing the damage requires reeling individual rights out of daily interactions and back into the role of protecting against unlawful coercion. This requires that judges, when faced with claimed violations of rights, must make legal rulings that protect the reasonable freedoms of everyone in society who might be involved in similar situations. This requires a shift in judges' conception of their role: instead of acting as referees in a private dispute, they must affirmatively defend boundaries of everyday freedom.

Expanding judicial responsibility to protect reasonable freedoms will be a dramatic change, but is essential to removing the legal Sword of Damocles that hangs over daily choices in America. This shift in judicial responsibility is not merely better policy, but, as I now describe, should be required as a matter of due process under any coherent conception of the rule of law.

Sue-for-anything justice weaponizes law as a tool for extortion. Conventional wisdom in America—contrary to the practice of every other Western legal system—is that people have a "right to sue" and have the case decided by a civil jury. As a result, pervasive distrust and defensiveness have supplanted everyday freedom. Teachers no longer will hug a crying child or restrain a student who is misbehaving. Hospitals and doctors practice defensive medicine, wasting upwards of $200 billion or more each year and compromising patient care by discouraging transparency. Parents impede the emotional growth of children by hovering over play dates and not letting children do things on their own.

Since the turn of the last century, prominent jurists Oliver Wendell Holmes, Jr., Benjamin Cardozo, Roger Traynor, and others have argued for predictable legal boundaries on lawsuits. The role of the civil jury should be to decide disputed issues of fact, such as who is telling the truth or who ran the red light. Standards of conduct, on the other hand, should be decided by judicial rulings that can be predictably applied from case to case. As Holmes put it:

> Negligence . . . [is] a standard of conduct, a standard which we hold the parties bound to know beforehand . . . not a matter dependent upon the whim of the particular jury or the eloquence of the particular advocate.

The flaw is not with juries, which are impartial and generally sensible. But jury verdicts make no rulings and set no precedent, so today no one has any sense of the boundaries of unreasonable behavior. In one case, the jury may find no liability. In a similar case, another jury may find liability. There's no legal boundary people can rely upon.

Even before the 1960s, it was a common judicial practice to throw all issues to juries. But the rights revolution supercharged the legal culture, adding an outrage factor to personal misfortune and inspiring a kind of feeding frenzy by trial lawyers. With the perfect vision of hindsight, any accident could have been prevented. Why didn't the manufacturer provide a warning that a soda bottle can pop if heated? Why didn't the Little League coach provide sunglasses to the outfielder? Outrage opened the door to huge claims for "pain and suffering" and punitive damages untethered to any knowable standard. What would you take to lose an eye? Or a loved one? Is $100 million enough? Maybe a little more?

No one thought much about the social costs of justice without legal boundaries. Tort reformers agitated for limits on noneconomic damages such as for "pain and suffering," but did not focus on how uncontrolled lawsuits corrode freedom with defensiveness. The availability of a possible claim, not an actual lawsuit, is what freezes intuitions needed for sensible everyday choices. "An act is illegal," Professor Donald Black noted, "if it is *vulnerable* to legal action."

Every other civilized country knows why judges must draw boundaries of reasonable claims. In a famous 2003 case, the high court in England dismissed a verdict against a county park where a young man suffered a tragic accident when he dove into a lake. Letting the verdict stand, the law lords held, would result in closure of lakes and rivers around the country and deny citizens the enjoyment of nature. "Does the law require that all trees be cut down because some youths may climb them and fall? Of course there is some risk of accidents . . . But that is no reason for imposing a gray and dull safety regime on everyone." It is the job of judges, as Lord Leonard Hoffmann stated, to make legal rulings that weigh "the social value of the activity which gives rise to the risk" and to dismiss claims involving risks that people should be free to take.

America is different, goes the retort, because the Constitution guarantees the right to jury trial. But the better view of the Seventh Amendment is that the jury in a civil case should resolve disputed factual issues—such as who is telling the truth—not decide legal standards on what is a valid claim. As future Chief Justice John Marshall put it during the constitutional debates: "What is the object of a jury trial? To inform the Court of the facts."

Trial lawyers trumpet the "right to sue" as an act of freedom, as if any accident victim or aggrieved person has the right to sue almost anyone in almost any amount and take the case to final verdict. In one crazy case in Washington, DC, a few years ago, the judge oversaw a trial in which the plaintiff sought $54 million against his dry cleaners for losing a pair of pants. The litigation lasted two years. The dry cleaners prevailed, of course, but defending the case put them through hell and the legal costs caused them to lose one of their two stores. In a less absurd context, the cost of defending products liability claims often drives companies to make huge settlements even in weak cases. RAND Corporation found that 90 percent of claimants in asbestos liability cases had no cancer, and most had no work-impairing symptoms.

What's needed is not to bar the courthouse door. Like other legal choices, deciding what's a reasonable claim requires a judgment in context. The missing element is that judges are not acting as gatekeepers at the outset of cases, keeping claims within reasonable bounds and thereby restoring public confidence in justice. In the lost pants lawsuit, it would have taken the judge about five minutes in a preliminary hearing to make this ruling: "Maybe you have a claim in small claims court for a few hundred dollars, but not for millions in a court of general jurisdiction. Case dismissed, without prejudice to refiling in small claims court."

Suing someone is not an act of freedom like, say, free speech. A lawsuit is a tool of state power, coming down to a verdict after which the sheriff can come and take your home away. A judge would never permit a prosecutor to seek the death penalty for a misdemeanor. So why do judges permit any aggrieved person to invoke state power for unreasonable claims in unlimited amounts against other free citizens?

Americans take pride that our system of justice is impartial, but impartiality, while essential, is not the main element of the rule of law. Law is not law if its boundaries are not generally predictable. The "basic moral principle, acknowledged by every legal system we know anything about," law professor Eugene Rostow observed, is "that similar cases should be decided alike." Citizens will not feel free to act on their best judgment unless they have reasonable notice of what and how much they can be sued for. Under American civil justice, people have no idea what or how much they can be sued for. That's why justice infects everyday freedom with distrust, imposes an unnecessary tax on commerce, and is widely derided by knowledgeable observers in other democratic countries.

I know that American justice has worked this way for a long time. But think about it: American courts allow lawsuits that are unconstrained by predictable legal norms and are decided without any concern for consistency. Except for our long acquiescence to this laissez-faire approach to lawsuits, it's hard to see how this conception of civil justice survives even cursory scrutiny under the constitutional requirements of due process.

It's easy to understand why Americans, after the turbulent 1960s, embraced a legal framework that promised to replace arguments over fairness with clear rules, objective processes, and rights for anyone who felt aggrieved. But law without human control only fueled the fires of distrust and discontent. The dream of automatic law was always hopeless. "Laws on paper are meaningless," legal historian Lawrence Friedman stated categorically: "they must be enforced or applied."

A principles-based legal framework that re-empowers human responsibility is the key structural solution for reviving everyday freedom. But, as I discuss now, we can't get there, or inspire a flourishing society, without also restoring the conditions for mutual trust.

VI.

REBUILDING TRUST FOR A FLOURISHING SOCIETY

Everyday freedom requires not only a zone of protected autonomy, but also trust that other people will abide by the reasonable values of society. Social trust is impossible unless people with institutional authority actively assert and enforce social norms.

Mutual trust is the lubricant of social interaction. When the people and institutions you deal with are trustworthy, you feel free to focus your energy on your goals and not be overly cautious. We don't fear being cheated if we trust that cheaters will be held accountable. We don't fear that coworkers will slack off, and leave us holding the bag, when we trust that supervisors won't tolerate it.

Trust lets people dive into projects with other people, confident that they can adapt and act reasonably when faced with unforeseen circumstances. Trust avoids diverting energy into defensiveness. "Trust and similar values . . . have real, practical economic value," economist Kenneth Arrow concluded: among other things, trustworthy values "increase the efficiency of the system." The more trust, the more freedom. The more trust, the stronger the economy.

Trust can be derived from shared cultural norms. Tim Carney in *Alienated America* discusses thriving communities that have a common national or religious heritage, such as Mormons in Utah. "Tradition bound" societies, Friedrich Hayek observed, are generally productive because individuals "conform voluntarily to certain principles." Acting in antisocial ways in these communities is virtually unthinkable.

In communities and institutions without shared traditions, trust requires reliable enforcement of norms of right and wrong and managerial direction to keep things moving forward. "The most important principle for designing an ethical society," social psychologist Jonathan Haidt concludes, "is to *make sure that everyone's reputation is on the line all the time*, so that bad behavior will always bring bad consequences." In administering price controls during World War II, Chester Bowles estimated that a small percentage of firms would comply even without any enforcement, but that 75 percent of firms would comply only if they knew that there was an active program to catch cheaters.

Sanctions for bad behavior go part of the way to restoring trust. But America has a bigger problem: Post–1960s law is built on the explicit premise of distrust of institutional choices. The greater the official's responsibility, the more suspect the decision. Distrust of justice, as noted, has fostered a culture of defensiveness. Asked if they would trust justice if someone brought "a baseless claim," only 16 percent of Americans said yes.

Distrust of authority contributes to institutional failure because the people in charge are preoccupied with avoiding error and satisfying the lowest common denominator. Distrust of institutional authority also undermines the mutual trust among all participants, as I will shortly discuss. People lose confidence in each other when there's no one upholding shared values, and revert towards self-interest. What fills the vacuum of values are rules and rigid protocols. All these rules and processes in turn hatch a "culture of resistance," law professor Joel Handler found: "Instead of fostering cooperation, it destroys it."

Deception is another cost of distrust. When you can get in trouble for saying something true, or expressing an honest opinion, you clam up or mouth the party line. But people readily perceive lack of honesty in, say, the stilted language of political correctness. Building trust is impossible, philosopher Onora O'Neill argues, when people don't feel free to be honest or true to themselves. The deception is not limited to language but extends to action. Instead of making decisions based on what's right and sensible, people do what they think they can justify. Distrust grows, because people see through this as well.

Deception is a slippery slope. A parallel public narrative develops which, because it's untethered to honest opinion, readily becomes untethered to facts. This is what happens in totalitarian regimes, where "facts" are transparent falsehoods. The harm is not that people believe the false assertions, Hannah Arendt explained, but that "the sense by which we take our bearings in the real world . . . is being destroyed." The Orwellian parallels are hard to miss. We too are trained to "deny the evidence of your senses."

A public operating system grounded in distrust of authority has seeded a broad sense of repression and un-freedom. Every incentive to do what's right gets turned upside down. Distrust discourages constructive behavior, for example, because people realize that trust has not been placed in them. "The de-skilling of teachers produces a kind of 'de-willing,'" Barry Schwartz and Kenneth Sharpe note in *Practical Wisdom*, "taking the fight out of some good teachers and takes other good teachers out of the fight."

What's at stake, we tell ourselves, is merely making sure no one is acting badly—better safe than sorry. Distrust after the 1960s is not caution, however, but an inversion of the hierarchy of responsibility. It is the *job* of a school principal to decide who's not an effective teacher, and letting the principal do that job is what liberates all teachers from the de-skilling dictates. It is the *job* of a mayor to deliver services effectively. Putting responsibility in shackles, and removing the freedom of supervisors to be honest, makes distrust self-fulfilling.

What's needed is not blind trust of people with responsibility; trust is always provisional and contingent on actual trustworthy encounters. That's the idea behind the adage "trust but verify." But trust requires the presumption that people with institutional responsibility can do what they think is right, including enforcing norms of reasonable behavior.

Instead, inexorably, distrust has become a core American value. Where concerned citizens once focused on initiatives to meet challenges, they now challenge routine decisions for suspect motives and possibilities of failure.

How Distrust Takes Over a Culture

Distrust blocking official authority isn't grounded in a legitimate conception of functional government. It's more like a scab we pick at. Just as humans are naturally risk averse, so too we tend to exaggerate the risk of abuses of power. Instead of aspiring to progress, Americans since the 1960s aspire to blocking things. America has become what political scientist Francis Fukuyama calls a "vetocracy."

In *The Moral Basis of a Backward Society*, Edward Banfield describes a region in southern Italy where trust had disappeared. Neighbors feared each other, and the lack of cooperation reduced everyone to subsistence farming. Local officials refused outside aid because, with any reform proposal, everyone would assume they would skim off much of it. Distrust was not regretted by the inhabitants in Banfield's backward society—distrust had become the value that people believed in. Banfield describes a culture in which people *wallowed* in the distrust—punishing their children, for example, to teach them not to be truthful when talking with neighbors.

Americans also seem to be wallowing in distrust. In *Alienated America*, Tim Carney discusses how distrust, like a spreading infection, has caused many Americans to retreat into dark places of their imagination, finding a sick fellowship with others who want to believe the worst of others and are dedicated to stopping things. In *The Righteous Mind*, Jonathan Haidt explains how "extreme partisanship may be literally addictive." For some, Jonah Goldberg argues, distrust is a kind of parlor game for people who are bored. A huge segment of the media is dedicated to scratching the itch of distrust.

Distrust has always been a device of political opposition, but in recent decades distrust has become a headline goal of political movements. Stop the steal! Defund the police! Woke ideologies on campus spin out towards ever more remote theories of personal offense and injustice.

Pulling out of this downward spiral is impossible in a scrum where no one is in charge. Because distrust causes failure, it seems to have the power of accuracy.

America will continue to frustrate its citizens until we re-empower institutional authority to pursue public goals, uphold norms of reasonable behavior, and defend the freedom to be truthful. Someone must grab hold of the tiller.

It's Not That Hard: Let People Take Responsibility Again

Getting things done is still part of America's DNA. On June 11, 2023, a truck delivering 8,500 gallons of gasoline had an accident underneath an elevated section of I-95 in Philadelphia and burst into flame, causing a section of I-95 to collapse. Initial reports suggested that traffic in the Northeast Corridor would be snarled for months. Twelve days later, the highway was reopened.

The key to the speedy repair was that Pennsylvania Governor Josh Shapiro declared an emergency and suspended all regulations that "would in any way prevent, hinder, or delay necessary action." Overriding specific regulations and procedures let the state immediately hire a reputable local highway contractor to perform "extra work" on existing contracts, thus avoiding the need for competitive bids.

The quickest way to build temporary lanes on an elevated road is to pave on top of landfill, but twelve-thousand-plus tons of dirt and rock might cause underlying water and sewer mains to collapse. So Michael Carroll, the head of the state's Department of Transportation, proposed using recycled glass, one-sixth the weight. Based on this engineering assessment, the decision was made almost immediately, a deal was made with a nearby recycled glass company, and the site started receiving recycled glass deliveries around the clock. Procurement rules were ignored.

All these decisions, and more, require permits from numerous state and local agencies. Mr. Carroll spent his days at the site issuing or waiving permit requirements.

As the temporary repair neared completion, wet weather made delays likely because of the need to lay and cure the asphalt surface. So Secretary Carroll proposed using the road-drying fan from the nearby Pocono Raceway, which provided the fan without charge.

On June 23, twelve days after the accident, I-95 reopened. The way the highway got repaired was not a miracle. The people in charge simply took responsibility to get the job done, using common sense, existing commercial and community relationships, and a little creativity. "We showed . . . good government in action," Governor Shapiro declared.

This repair job was a big story because government doesn't usually work this way. Public contracting procedures, by trying to detail every conceivable contingency, often raise costs by multiples over similar private contracts. Permits can take years.

Why do Americans tolerate wasteful public systems? The answer is a reflexive distrust of public authority. What if the highway official is on the take? What if the governor wants to hire his buddy? Our collective instinct for distrust overrides waste, poor performance, and unaccountability.

Studies on public corruption, by contrast, recommend empowering identifiable officials to use their judgment instead of diluting responsibility in red tape. Giving authority to individual officials means everyone knows where to shine the light of accountability. That was the advice of the Framers as well. "The sole and undivided responsibility of one man will naturally beget a livelier sense of duty and a more exact regard to reputation," Alexander Hamilton advised. Otherwise, responsibility can be "shifted from one to another with so much dexterity, and under such plausible appearances, that the public opinion is left in suspense about the real author."

No society or institution has ever succeeded by declaring it irresponsible for people to take responsibility. Americans know how to do things. The exceptions prove the rule. The I-95 repair encountered no backbiting from distrust because of Americans' greater loathing of traffic jams. Ditto with "Operation Warp Speed," the multibillion dollar research project that gave us COVID-19 vaccines in less than six months.

In 2023, Baltimore found that in twenty-three public schools not one student was proficient in math. Not one. In Chicago, thirty-seven schools had not one student proficient in either math or reading. These schools need to be shaken up—new principals, new teachers, new anything. Because of system-imbedded distrust that someone might make a mistake, however, no one has the authority to reorganize these schools. Could it get any worse?

Restoring the conditions for mutual trust requires overcoming two taboos of modern law: People with responsibility must be empowered to assert norms of what's right and reasonable, and they must be free to make judgments about the people they work with.

Why Value Judgments Are Essential to Trust

Mutual trust requires a belief that other people will abide by the reasonable values of the institution or of society. But we also know that, left to their own devices, people tend to act in their self-interest. As discussed, rules and processes don't inspire mutual trust because rote compliance often offends common sense and can be gamed. So what is the mechanism for mutual trust?

Other than tradition, there is probably only one way to build social trust: Judges, officials, school principals, supervisors, and others with institutional authority must assert and enforce values of what's right and reasonable. In any organization, Peter Drucker noted, "there have to be people who make decisions . . . who are accountable for the organization's mission, its spirit, its performance, its results."

But letting responsible officials make what are known as "value judgments" is what modern law is designed to prevent. As a famous trial judge put it during the heyday of the rights revolution: "Choosing among values is much too important a business for judges to do the choosing. That is something the citizens must keep for themselves."

Nothing works sensibly or fairly unless people in charge can make value judgments. The annals of bureaucracy are filled with horror stories of paralysis, injustice, and worse because officials feel they are not authorized to act on their values of right and wrong. Environmental reviews are often interminable, for example, because officials won't make value judgments to limit what issues need to be analyzed. Many public schools have a culture like penal institutions because disciplinary and personnel decisions are disconnected from right and wrong—as with zero tolerance rules discussed earlier. Social workers suffer burnout or quit because of a sense they can't do what they know is right—such as when a toddler in a drug-addled household was electrocuted because the social worker was powerless to remove her until after a mandatory waiting period. Government procurement rules regularly result in poor products and staggering waste because the rules are designed to prevent officials from acting on their best judgment.

The 1960s quest for neutral governing was utopian. Value-free governance was never free of values.

The vacuum of authority created when judges and officials started sitting on their hands was quickly filled with the values of whoever wanted something. Like a kind of black magic, distrust of value judgments by officials transferred power to self-interested people. As legal scholar Robert Kagan explains: "The spirit of distrust of authority . . . can be used against the trustworthy too. An equal opportunity weapon, it can be used by the misguided, the mendacious, and the malevolent."

Social trust is impossible unless legal and public decisions are tethered to values of right and wrong. People don't have to agree with decisions, but they need to feel that officials are aspiring to do what's right. As Michael Lipsky observes in *Street-Level Bureaucracy*, trust in government requires officials "*at least to be open to the possibility* that each [situation] presents special circumstances."

Values when applying law are only the tip of the values needed for healthy institutions. What holds an institution together are values in daily interaction and implementation which can never be dictated in legal codes. In an *Atlantic* essay published in 1924, and then republished by the *Atlantic* in 1942, John Fletcher Moulton, a noted British judge and cabinet minister, discussed the separate "domain of human action" that exists between legal requirements and personal freedom. This is "the whole realm which recognizes the sway of duty, fairness, sympathy, taste, and all the other things that make life beautiful and society possible."

Columnist David Brooks writes powerfully about the need for moral education to reclaim "a community of common values, whose members aspire to earn one another's respect." The way to make morality real is not mainly through sermons, however, but, as I will discuss next, by accountability. People with institutional responsibility must have authority to assert and enforce those values if the institution is to succeed and foster individual pride. Governing without values "is too cold and formal to have a beneficial influence on society," Aleksandr Solzhenitsyn said in a 1978 Harvard commencement address, "and creates an atmosphere of spiritual mediocrity that paralyzes man's noblest impulses."

Value judgments needed to run an institution will be much more personal than the legal value judgments needed to enforce the boundaries of judicial enforcement. But justice too will not be trusted until judges and officials assert norms of reasonableness when applying law. As Justice Cardozo explained, the judge must be "the interpreter for the community of its sense of law and order":

> The judge is under a duty . . . to maintain a relation between law and morals, between the precepts of jurisprudence and those of reason and good conscience . . . This is judicial

legislation, and the judge legislates at his peril. Nevertheless, it is the necessity and duty of such legislation that gives to judicial office its highest honor.

VII.

INSTITUTIONAL AUTHORITY IS VITAL TO EVERYDAY FREEDOM

Society doesn't deliver goods and services automatically. America works through institutions such as businesses, schools, hospitals, public departments, colleges, and charities. They are the vehicles for social achievement. Their strength translates directly into our strength. That is reason enough to reset the rules that hobble institutional authority.

Institutional authority is also critical for individual freedom. The institutions of society are the springboards for individuals to make a difference. An individual can strap into the institutional vehicle with the engine already running. An institution provides the purpose, and the resources, and the values of interaction needed to enable people to pull together. By obviating the need to think through countless assumptions and issues, institutions empower people to focus on achieving higher goals. Ideas accelerate, economist Paul Romer found, as each new idea empowers all participants to advance further.

For institutions to work effectively, both for society and for the individuals within them, institutions must have the authority to sustain standards of excellence and trust. Judgments about accountability are critical, not only concerning particular employees but also to build mutual trust that everyone is committed to the values of the organization and to excellence. There's hardly anything more corrosive to an organization than the knowledge that performance doesn't matter.

Law after the 1960s puts managerial authority into a suspect category, similar to protecting against the coercive power of the state. The goal was to protect individuals against unfair or biased decisions by supervisors, but weakening institutional authority had the paradoxical effect of weakening the freedoms and opportunities of individuals. Protocols replaced initiative. Behavior codes replaced spontaneity. An entire industry for morality training aims to safeguard employers from legal claims by sterilizing human interaction. In the land of the First Amendment, professors are afraid to continue conversations on a campus elevator because there's no way to draw the line on words or ideas that might offend someone.

For an individual employee, the spirit of the workplace is critical. The department's spirit is reflected in its energy, and its sense of mission, and its receptivity to quality. In *Practical Wisdom*, Schwartz and Sharpe write about the pride of custodial workers in hospitals who see their job not only as cleaning, but as being sensitive to the needs of patients and family members—for example, not vacuuming when family members of patients are napping in the waiting room. It makes a huge difference to any joint endeavor, psychologist Amy Wrzesniewski and colleagues found, when employees see their work as a "calling" instead of a "job."

The human qualities that instill purpose, pride, and trust are not susceptible to objective criteria such as metrics. As Schwartz and Sharpe describe, flourishing requires "character traits like loyalty, self-control, courage, fairness, generosity, gentleness, friendliness, and truthfulness," as well as "perseverance, integrity, open-mindedness, thoroughness, and kindness."

Individual engagement in their work, and the ability to work with others who are similarly engaged, is where many people find meaning and happiness. When observing an inspiring teacher, Philip Jackson and colleagues found that "the most important thing" she communicates is that she "likes being where she is and doing what she's doing."

An institution committed to excellence inspires "a readiness to perceive and act." By contrast, no person with pride wants to work in a place where people barely go through the motions. "We note deep disaffection within the public service," the 2003 Volcker Commission concluded. "An outmoded personnel system . . . keeps them from fully developing or utilizing their talents. They resent the protections provided to those poor performers among them who impede their own work and drag down the reputation of all government workers."

How should judgments about people be made? They're more akin to moral judgments, based on perceptions that are hard to articulate. People know it when they see it, but they can't spell it out. In *The Moral Life of Schools*, Philip Jackson and colleagues describe how we make these judgments: "Laying aside all exceptions to the rule, there is typically a lot of truth in the judgments we make of others. And this is so even when we cannot quite put our finger on the source of our opinion. That truth, we would suggest, *emerges expressively*. It is given off by what a person says and does, the way a smile gives off an aura of friend-liness or tears a spirit of sadness." Impressions about people rarely change, psychologist Jonathan Haidt found, even after "much longer and more leisurely observation and deliberation."

But what if the supervisor is prejudiced, or has inappropriate motives? Nowhere is distrust more raw than when evaluating other people. Although we know that managers of sports teams often need to change the lineup to get results, we view with suspicion that same authority in the workplace and other settings. Political scientist Alan Wolfe, in his study of American values, found that there is "an Eleventh Commandment: Thou shalt not judge." The instinct for job security is timeless, and avoiding high-handed and discriminatory prac-tices is now a universal value in modern society. But it is not hard to impose reasonable speed bumps to pro-tect against unfairness—such as, say, a parent-teacher committee in a school, or worker councils that some manufacturers consult to review terminations. Making supervisors run a legal gauntlet to make personnel choices, on the other hand, undermines the mutual trust that all will be held to high standards.

The ultimate objection to being "judgmental" is that it violates the person's rights. But this argument is obviously circular. What about the rights of the students stuck in schools where no one is proficient in reading or math? Or the rights of good teachers who are shackled to rigid course plans designed for inept teachers? Or, indeed, the rights of citizens who spend more on public schools than any other country, with miserable results?

A culture of excellence and pride cannot be reconciled with the fear of making personnel judgments. People are indeed different from each other. Hayek noted the "boundless variety of human nature," and Arendt discussed the "unlikeness" of every person "to all other people we know." But this personal uniqueness means that some people will be better at certain things than at others and may do well in one setting and not in another. Fidelity to the common culture is another criterion where individuals will differ. Some people will act inappropriately and should be let go. For all these reasons, judgments about people are vital to the success of both the institution and all the other individuals within it.

It's a mistake to treat jobs as fine china. Most employees are "neither good nor bad," management expert Chester Barnard observed, "but only good or bad in this or that position." There are millions of workplaces in America. Each of these workplaces has its own culture and way of doing things. It is the job of supervisors to decide who's doing the job and who's not. Coworkers are the main beneficiaries of honest personnel choices. It would be far preferable, and less costly, to adopt a "flexicurity" program like that in Denmark—where terminated employees get up to two years of income support—than to corrode workplace culture by retaining employees who don't pull their weight. Similarly, it would be far preferable to terminate employees who act inappropriately than to discourage honest interaction under stultifying speech codes.

Institutions are the vehicles which provide goods and services for our society and propel it forward. How well these institutions work is determined largely by their ability to marshal human resources towards the institutional goals. Key factors for success include energy, skill, shared values, and coordination of the individual employees and managers. Mutual trust is essential, or all those factors for success soon dissipate. Trust within institutions can fail for many reasons, but the surest route is to prevent judgments on accountability. Mutual trust requires confidence that everyone is pulling hard, or else will be asked to leave. Everyone must believe that performance matters. The freedom to judge other participants, and the exposure to being judged, are foundational conditions for a healthy institution.

VIII.

COMMUNITY RESPONSIBILITY
AND SOCIAL COHESION

The human need for agency—to feel that our ideas and effort make a difference—is expressed not only in our families and workplaces. It is also expressed in our community activities, with neighbors, with the PTA and Little League, with the church or synagogue, and with local charities and government. Tocqueville considered "the art of associating together" to be essential "if men are to remain civilized."

Community activities keep people's feet on the ground as citizens engage with real human needs and differences. Working together in community projects builds "social capital," sociologist Robert Putnam describes, reinforcing "norms of reciprocity and trustworthiness." Alienation vanishes when people have personal agency and cooperate with others in joint projects. Differences in values are trumped by practical needs. When dealing with concrete situations, studies show, people with polarized political views will often reach similar conclusions. The "point of civil society," sociologist James Davison Hunter observes, "is to provide mediating institutions to stand between the individual and the state, or the individual and the economy. They're at their best when they are doing just that: They are mediating, they are educating . . . [T]he alternatives are violence."

People in isolation, by contrast, readily go off the deep end. Without a sense of belonging, solitary people are susceptible to abstract thinking that readily spins into extremism. Social media amplifies these worst tendencies of human nature, reinforcing nihilistic ideas and fantasies. The appalling regularity of shootings in schools, churches, and synagogues are perpetrated by individuals isolated in their own nightmare worlds.

The decline of community after the 1960s was prominently chronicled by sociologist Robert Putnam in *Bowling Alone*. The causes include what observers call "workism," when both parents work hard and lack the energy to do more. Centralized regulation imposes another impediment to community activities—for example, banning home-cooked meals from food pantries because the state inspector couldn't certify home kitchens. Mother Teresa abandoned plans to build a shelter for the homeless in a three-story building in the Bronx because no one had authority to waive the code requirement for an expensive elevator. The overhang of possible legal exposure smothers local initiative—for example, resulting in cancelling a Little League game because paid umpires didn't show, and volunteer parent umpires might, well, who knows, make the wrong call.

What put community on life support was the outsourcing of social services to distant government bureaucracies. Communities lost the moral imperative and the resources to help those in need. My father was a minister in small towns in the South, and I tagged along when he went to prison work camps and organized parishioners for food pantries and other social services. Today, the responsibility of local citizens to provide services through intermediate social institutions—schools, churches, and charities—has become largely supplanted by state bureaucracies.

The hollowing out of communities occurred gradually. As central government departments took over local activities, churches lost membership, civic associations such as the Rotary Club faded away, and new generations lost the habit of joining with others to improve their community. The effect, as social philosopher Yuval Levin describes in *The Fractured Republic*, is that American society resembles a dumbbell—with centralized government and regulations on one end and isolated individuals on the other end. Tocqueville thought that if "an American were condemned to confine his activity to his own affairs, he would be robbed of one half of his existence." Today, the idea of active community life is a quaint historical reference to barn-raisings and John Philip Sousa concerts in a gazebo.

Freedom has instead been defined as a solitary activity—the "right to be left alone." Conceiving of "human beings as rights-bearing individuals who could pursue their own understanding of the good life," Matthew Rose puts it in *A World After Liberalism*, is an "impoverished . . . picture of human life," which ignores that humans "are social creatures who find meaning through relationships," including bonds of family and community "they have not chosen." Taking responsibility for those around us is not done for personal pleasure but for personal meaning and self-respect.

Rebuilding communities requires a deliberate policy change to shift responsibility to local agencies, religious groups, and charities. Our economy represents what we value. If we value centralized bureaucracy, or flat-screened TVs, or big stone heads, then we'll direct resources in those directions. If we value community activities, we need to give them authority and resources.

Many of the institutions still exist and can be revitalized. Churches, despite their decline, are still the largest and most important institution of civil society. The prospect of joining with others and making a difference will lure many people away from the disembodied interactions online. Reviving community services also adds opportunities for responsible jobs—for example, staffing assisted living facilities for the homeless, and organizing parenting sessions for single mothers and their infants to try to break multigenerational cycles of poverty.

Reviving the role of churches and local charities does not require romanticizing the good old days. Enlarging public aid programs liberated many people in need from dependence on charity. Government income support for a poor family, for example, provides more agency and dignity to a needy family than a food pantry. But social services are still needed. These involve real people, with specific needs, who aren't well served by "mindless application of harsh rules [and] people treated as objects" that is common with centralized bureaucracies. Many of these services could be organized effectively by local agencies, churches, and charities, including, in addition to assisted living for the homeless and tutoring, other after-school programs, care for the elderly, job apprenticeships, and prisoner reentry assistance.

The path back to community leadership is not through hortatory appeals to do good but through empowerment. Giving communities "power and independence," Tocqueville noted, is the prerequisite for "active citizens." Authority has a gravitational force, pulling people in because they see an opportunity to make a difference or because they have different ideas. Giving local organizations the authority and resources to provide services their own way will awaken the interest of others in the community.

The Ukrainian mobilization to repel the Russian invasion in 2022, political scientist Jennifer Murtazashvili concluded, can be attributed in part to a decision by Ukrainian government in 2014 to devolve significant decision-making authority to mayors and councils of Ukraine towns and cities. Lines of authority and trust in local communities were well established by 2022, and could be drawn upon to mount resistance, collect and disseminate intelligence, and avoid panic and capitulation.

Most Americans no longer have the memory of what an active community can achieve. A bad school, or rogue cop, would not be tolerated in a community where citizens and officials are empowered to make changes.

Wherever practical, government should delegate services and provide resources to credible local groups, and provide block grants conditioned on performance. Just as officials in Pennsylvania used their judgment to rebuild the fallen section of I-95 in twelve days, so too local officials and charities should be judged by how they do, not told how to do it. Dense bureaucracy is impossible for volunteers to navigate. Reengaging citizens requires letting them do things in their own ways. Just as law sets outer boundaries, government should see its job as evaluating performance and guarding against waste and misconduct. What matters is results, not compliance.

Distrust rears its head again: People will be suspicious that volunteers for church social services will try to advance their religious beliefs. What if a volunteer talks about his religious faith? Where public moneys are involved, I would support a general principle against religious proselytizing. But the benefits of community ownership of social services vastly outweigh, in my view, the harms of religious affiliation. Churches and synagogues should not be kept on the sidelines of society on the logic of separating church and state.

It is ironic, of course, that political activists who demand neutral values are actually demanding conformity with their own values. The post–1960s idea of law as a precision tool for correct behavior readily spawns demands to end wrong thinking forever, or at least one group's conception of it. The ideal of a tolerant society has been replaced by a kind of one-correct-view fundamentalism. Cancel culture is not a big step from the self-centered conception of individual rights: Rights for me but not for thee. As a young professor told a group at a lunch I attended, without irony: "There's no such thing as cancel culture. It's just that some people are wrong."

A free society should honor communities of different values, within a broad range, and encourage like-minded people to come together to find purpose in taking responsibility for local needs and services. This should be a national priority, because, as Tocqueville warned, the purpose of society has been "lost to [our] senses." Making people partakers in local affairs, he thought, is the "most powerful and perhaps the only means" of escaping from the alienation that is draining the vitality of our culture.

IX.

THE FREEDOM TO SAVE OURSELVES

America is suffering from a crisis of human disempowerment. The legal framework built since the 1960s prevents people from taking responsibility and doing what we think is right. Government is failing for the same reason it has estranged its citizens. It preempts the active intelligence and moral judgments of people on the ground.

Americans haven't revolted to overthrow this anti-human system, I've come to understand, because we focus on how to create a better system instead of restoring the primacy of human judgment. Our aspiration for system solutions is the problem—as Havel put it, we're searching for "an objective way out of the crisis of objectivism." Like the people chained deep in Plato's cave, we are deluded into thinking that the shadows of legal machinations represent the real tools of governance.

What's missing is belief in our own beliefs. Doing what's right and sensible requires individual judgments by the responsible person. That's what taking responsibility means—making value judgments, not avoiding them; taking risks where needed, not avoiding them; aspiring to a better world, not clinging to the status quo.

The hands-free governing system is taking America towards a cliff. The important question should be not "what does the rule require?" but "what does this situation need?" Instead we go where the system takes us, lemming-like, notwithstanding the clear trail of failures. We don't bail out because we literally can't conceive of humans doing what they think is right. The theology of law better than people has been drummed into our heads as virtuous.

We see I-95 get fixed in twelve days, and COVID-19 vaccines created in a matter of months, but are taught that a system built on distrust of human judgment, including our own, is proof of our moral probity.

Everyday freedom requires not so much a reform as a complete change in direction—akin to the Progressive Era's abandonment of laissez-faire. The operating philosophy of everyday freedom reclaims founding principles of human responsibility—a nation which is "designated by Providence," in George Washington's words, "for the display of human greatness and felicity." Freedom is supposed to allow people "'to make the best of themselves,'" Isaiah Berlin explained.

By reviving human agency, everyday freedom will remove many of the causes of alienation. It also will create the conditions for good government because, as

Peter Drucker observed, "a free society rests on the freedom to make responsible decisions." Elevating the role of human judgment opens the door to an infinitude of new solutions. Fresh judgment, unlike frozen bureaucratic dictates, can move mountains. "The whole world's future hangs on a proper judgment," General George Marshall said after World War II, "of what can best be done, on what must be done."

I don't minimize the political difficulty of changing the legal operating system. But this shift, I believe, is not optional. We watch the social fabric fray and get weaker every year. America can't get where we want, and Americans can't be who we want, with a governing structure designed for human disempowerment.

The impetus for big change must be overwhelming public demand. This requires a clear vision: It is "necessary to be bold," Thomas Paine wrote, to inspire people to "begin to think." It usually also takes a crisis to provoke public demand, as with the Great Depression prompting the New Deal, and the civil rights movement and antiwar protests sparking the 1960s rights revolution. When the shift of opinion towards change happens, it's almost unstoppable: "There is an amazing strength in the expression of the will of a whole people," Tocqueville observed.

The only practical mechanism for designing new frameworks is for Congress to delegate the design of structures, area by area, to independent recodification commissions. Then the proposals can be put to a vote by Congress, weighing the costs and benefits of the overall package. That's more or less how new legal codes have been adopted through history.

The greatest hurdle to change will be repudiating the current governing philosophy. The post–1960s legal system sits on our cultural altar—dedicated to a self-interested concept of individual rights and to the eradication of human error and injustice. Generations of lawmakers since the 1960s have tried to perfect it. Instead, it pulverizes public goals as well as the human spirit.

The failure of modern law was baked into its founding premise—to enhance freedom by replacing human authority. Thick rulebooks and processes guarantee failure, not fairness. Demands for individual rights against powerful institutions have enormous rhetorical power. But those institutions are the arenas within which most people exercise our freedom. Schools, hospitals, workplaces, universities, and public agencies should work for the benefit of all, not at the point of a legal gun for the benefit of a few.

Authority is not the enemy of freedom; it provides the sentries that define and protect freedom. Your own freedom to make reasonable choices is contingent upon the authority of judges and officials to draw these boundaries. Morality in the public sphere is impossible without authority. Freedom itself is a concept of authority—the authority to do things your own way.

At the end of his life, Friedrich Hayek reconsidered "the supposed greater certainty [when] . . . all rules of law have been laid down in written and codified form." He concluded that "I am now persuaded . . . that judicial decisions may in fact be more predictable if the judge is also bound by generally held views of what is just, even when they are not supported by the letter of the law." Law's effectiveness, Hayek concluded, hinges on its ability to stay aligned with social norms: "The rule of law is effective . . . only insofar as it is part of the moral tradition of the community."

We too must confront the failure of our accepted wisdom. We created this elaborate legal machinery with noble intentions. But we now know that it's not possible to create a government better than people. Modern law fails because it is dehumanizing, and, however hard this may prove to be, it must be replaced by a framework that empowers everyday freedom.

NOTES

Introduction

1 Ken Wagner: Conversation with author, July 13, 2023; Linda Borg and Madeleine List, "Schools Superintendent to Step Down," *The Providence Journal*, February 26, 2019.

2 "systemic issues in our healthcare system": Jesse M. Ehrenfeld, "Burnout Is Causing Doctors to Leave Medicine. Here's How to Help Them Stay," *The Boston Globe*, July 13, 2023.

2 A sense of futility: See discussion in Philip K. Howard, *The Collapse of the Common Good: How America's Lawsuit Culture Undermines Our Freedom* (New York: Ballantine, 2001), 128–31. "I feel very unimportant," a social worker confided to Studs Terkel. "Success is to be in a position where I can make a decision." Studs Terkel, *Working: People Talk About What They Do All Day and How They Feel About What They Do* (New York: New Press, 1997), 343. See generally Philip K. Howard, *Not Accountable: Rethinking the Constitutionality of Public Employee Unions* (Garden City, NY: Rodin, 2023).

2 "learn they can't make a difference": Conversation by author with David Maloney. See discussion in *The Collapse of the Common Good*, 114–31. Political scientist Daniel DiSalvo tells the story of a female painter from the Facilities Department at City College of New York who, having seen DiSalvo talk on television, stopped by on her coffee break to discuss her frustrations with work restrictions: "She couldn't believe how much time it took to do anything . . . She couldn't stand the detailed rules. She felt insulted because they didn't allow her to prove how fast and how talented a painter she was. The combination of unionization and government employment was undermining her pride in her craft." Daniel DiSalvo, *Government Against Itself: Public Union Power and Its Consequences* (New York: Oxford University Press, 2015), 25–26. See also Leisha DeHart-Davis and Sanjay

87

K. Pandey, "Red Tape and Public Employees," *Journal of Public Administration Research and Theory*, May 2009.

2 This is one reason: See, e.g., Rachel Feintzeig, "U.S. Struggles to Draw Young, Savvy Staff," *The Wall Street Journal*, June 10, 2014: "The government's reputation for bureaucracy and hierarchy is driving away many workers, says Paul Light, a professor of public policy at New York University . . . 'The federal government used to be an employer of choice,' he says, 'and now it's an employer of last resort.'" See also The National Commission on Public Service, "Urgent Business for America: Revitalizing the Federal Government for the 21st Century," January 2003, iv: "Too few of our most talented citizens are seeking careers in government . . . The difficulties federal workers encounter in just getting their jobs done has led to discouragement and low morale."

3 "growing majority of Americans": James Davison Hunter, "How America's Culture Wars Have Evolved into a Class War," *The Washington Post*, September 12, 2017.

3 "a threat to [our] existence": Professor Hunter is quoted in Zack Stanton, "How the 'Culture War' Could Break Democracy," *Politico Magazine*, May 20, 2021.

3 "self-interest, rightly understood": Alexis de Tocqueville, *Democracy in America*, ed. Phillips Bradley (New York: Vintage, 1990), 1:393.

4 For several decades: See generally media, interviews, and reviews collected at www.commongood.org and www.philipkhoward.com.

4 Many Americans no longer believe in America: See, e.g., The University of Chicago Institute of Politics, "Our Precarious Democracy: Extreme Polarization and Alienation in Our Politics," June 29, 2022, 1: "A majority of Americans agree that the government is 'corrupt and rigged against everyday people like me,'" and "nearly half of Americans (49 percent) agreed that they 'more and more feel like a stranger in my own country.'"

I. The Human Need to Do Things Our Own Way

7 "'individual power,' the capacity to act": Eric Foner, *The Story of American Freedom* (New York: W.W. Norton, 1998), 53, quoting John Quincy Adams. See also Isaiah Berlin, *Four Essays on Liberty* (Oxford: Oxford University Press, 1969), ix: "[T]o be free to choose, and not to be chosen for, is an inalienable ingredient of what makes human beings human."

8 Individual responsibility was replaced by red tape and legal process: See generally Philip K. Howard, "From Progressivism to Paralysis," 130 *The Yale Law Journal Forum* 370 (January 2021); Philip K. Howard, *The Rule of Nobody: Saving America from Dead Laws and Broken Government* (New York: W.W. Norton, 2014); and Philip K. Howard, *Try Common Sense: Replacing the Failed Ideologies of Right and Left* (New York: W.W. Norton, 2019).

9 Selfishness has filled the vacuum: See David Brooks, "How America Got Mean," *The Atlantic*, August 14, 2023: "Our society has become one in which people feel licensed to give their selfishness free rein."

9 "It is especially dangerous": Alexis de Tocqueville, *Democracy in America*, ed. Phillips Bradley (New York: Vintage, 1990), 2:320.

II. Everyday Freedom Is Essential for Achievement

11 "nine-tenths of all organization activity": Chester Irving Barnard, *The Functions of the Executive* (Cambridge, MA: Harvard University Press, 1968), 232. For examples of the importance of public decisions on the spot, see Michael Lipsky, *Street-Level Bureaucracy: Dilemmas of the Individual in Public Services* (New York: Russell Sage, 1980) and Philip W. Jackson, Robert E. Boostrom, and David T. Hansen, *The Moral Life of Schools* (San Francisco: Jossey-Bass, 1998).

11 artificial intelligence: See, e.g., Joe McKendrick and Andy Thurai, "AI Isn't Ready to Make Unsupervised Decisions," *Harvard Business Review*, September 15, 2022, and "Pause Giant AI Experiments: An Open Letter," Future of Life Institute, March 22, 2023.

13 "most elementary manifestation": Hannah Arendt, "What Is Authority?," in *The Portable Hannah Arendt* (New York: Penguin, 2003), 466.

13 This is for cognitive reasons: See generally Michael Polanyi, *Personal Knowledge: Towards a Post-Critical Philosophy* (Chicago: University of Chicago Press, 1962); Gerd Gigerenzer, *Gut Feelings: The Intelligence of the Unconscious* (New York: Penguin, 2008); Mike

Rose, *The Mind at Work: Valuing the Intelligence of the American Worker* (New York: Viking, 2004); Malcolm Gladwell, *Blink: The Power of Thinking Without Thinking* (Boston: Back Bay, 2007); and Kenneth R. Hammond, *Human Judgment and Social Policy: Irreducible Uncertainty, Inevitable Error, Unavoidable Injustice* (New York: Oxford University Press, 1996).

13   "disappear . . . into the task": Rose, *The Mind at Work*, 112.

13   Our knowledge is in our action: See Polanyi, *Personal Knowledge*, 267: "Our mind lives in action."

14   "did not sit in airplanes": William Langewiesche, *Fly by Wire: The Geese, the Glide, the Miracle on the Hudson* (New York: Farrar, Straus and Giroux, 2009), 177.

14   "The earth and the river": Capt. Chesley "Sully" Sullenberger, "What I Got Back," *Parade*, October 11, 2009.

14   A pianist cannot play the piece: Polanyi, *Personal Knowledge*, 56.

14   For activities that involve sensory or personal taste: See, e.g., Gladwell, *Blink*, 179–81. A study on consumer ability to discern popular taste in jam found that the group required to explain their reasons made worse choices than those who simply made a judgment without reasons.

14   "The Emotional Dog and Its Rational Tail": Jonathan Haidt, "The Emotional Dog and its Rational Tail: A Social Intuitionist Approach to Moral Judgment," 108 *Psychological Review* 814 (2001).

14   But human decision-making: See Daniel Kahneman, *Thinking, Fast and Slow* (New York: Farrar, Straus and Giroux, 2011). See also Cass R. Sunstein, Daniel Kahneman, and Olivier Sibony, *Noise: A Flaw in Human Judgment* (New York: Little, Brown, 2021).

15   rule-of-thumb protocols: Gerd Gigerenzer and Julian Marewski tell how a simple decision tree with three questions was far more effective than complex algorithms for emergency room doctors to better sort out potential cardiac patients. Julian N. Marewski and Gerd Gigerenzer, "Heuristic Decision Making in Medicine" 14 *Dialogues in Clinical Neuroscience* 77 (March 2012), Figure 1.

15   A rote checklist: See, e.g., Philip K. Howard, "Problems with Protocols," *The Wall Street Journal*, January 20, 2010 (review of Atul

Gawande's *The Checklist Manifesto: How to Get Things Right* [New York: Metropolitan, 2009]).

15 **"rationalist delusion"**: Jonathan Haidt, *The Righteous Mind: Why Good People Are Divided by Politics and Religion* (New York: Vintage, 2013), 103–06.

15 **"usual process of unconscious trial and error"**: Polanyi, *Personal Knowledge*, 62.

15 **"The Dog and the Frisbee"**: Andrew Haldane, "The Dog and the Frisbee," presentation to the Federal Reserve Bank of Kansas City, August 31, 2012, available at https://www.bankofengland. co.uk/-/media/boe/files/paper/2012/the-dog-and-the-frisbee.pdf.

15 **"intuitive powers"**: Polanyi, *Personal Knowledge*, 130. The unconscious nature of creativity and innovation doesn't mean it's not the product of training, hard work, and experience. But all that effort is put together in the unconscious, not by conscious reasoning. See Polanyi, *Personal Knowledge*, 106: "For the capacity for making discoveries is not a kind of gambler's luck. It depends on natural ability, fostered by training and guided by intellectual effort. It is akin to artistic achievement and like it is unspecifiable."

16 **reasoning is used to rationalize intuitions**: Haidt, "The Emotional Dog and Its Rational Tail," 822. Haidt, *The Righteous Mind*, 47–51.

16 **"amazingly few people"**: Peter F. Drucker, *The Peter F. Drucker Reader: Selected Articles from the Father of Modern Management Thinking* (Boston: Harvard Business Review, 2016), 141.

16 **the process of trial and error**: "Nothing that's any good works by itself, just to please you," Thomas Edison said: "You got to make the damn thing work." Neil Baldwin, *Edison: Inventing the Century* (Chicago: University of Chicago Press, 2001), 296.

16 **Taking responsibility**: Barnard, *The Functions of the Executive*, 267: "*The point is that responsibility is the property of an individual by which whatever morality exists in him becomes effective in conduct.*" (Emphasis in original.)

16 **Everyday freedom operates in a kind of marketplace**: Observing and forming opinions about other people is a continuous human activity. Hayek referred to this as the "principle of rewarding a man according to what others think": "How faithfully and intelligently . . . how well he has fitted himself into the whole machinery, must be determined by the opinion of other people." Friedrich A. Hayek, *The Constitution of Liberty*, ed. Ronald Hamowy (Chicago: University of Chicago Press, 2011), 188.

16   Like atoms in a test tube: Chester Barnard discusses the many reasons why people choose one place of work over another: "The question of personal compatibility or incompatibility is much more far-reaching in limiting cooperative effort than is recognized"; "Men often will not work at all, and will rarely work well, . . . if the social situation *from their point of view* is unsatisfactory." *The Functions of the Executive*, 146–47. See also Polanyi, *Personal Knowledge*, 210–21: "Conviviality is a key to group success."

16   Teachers who don't succeed: C. K. Jackson, "Match Quality, Worker Productivity, and Worker Mobility: Direct Evidence from Teachers," 95 *Review of Economics and Statistics* 1096 (2013) (finding that teachers who changed schools due to a poor "match" at their original school often improved their performance, and that "match quality" is one of the most important predictors of student achievement). See discussion in David Epstein, *Range: Why Generalists Triumph in a Specialized World* (New York: Riverhead, 2019), 132.

16   Law has a role to play: See discussion in Philip K. Howard, *The Collapse of the Common Good: How America's Lawsuit Culture Undermines Our Freedom* (New York: Ballantine, 2001), 173–98.

17   Studies show that trying too hard to purge bias: See, e.g., Alexandra Kalev, Frank Dobbin, Erin Kelly, "Best Practices or Best Guesses? Assessing the Efficacy of Corporate Affirmative Action and Diversity Policies," 71 *American Sociological Review* 589 (2006) (finding that attempts to limit managerial bias had the perverse effect of *increasing* managers' reliance on biased judgments). Some studies suggest that subjective evaluations are no more prone to bias than ones that seek objective ratification. See Gregory Mitchell and Philip E. Tetlock, "Antidiscrimination Law and the Perils of Mindreading," 67 *Ohio State Law Journal* 1023 (2006); Melissa Hart, "Subjective Decision-making and Unconscious Discrimination, 56 *Alabama Law Review* 741, 748 (2005).

17   Successful relationships require candor and mutual respect: See discussion in Howard, *The Collapse of the Common Good*, 173–98 and in Philip K. Howard, *Life Without Lawyers: Restoring Responsibility in America* (New York: W.W. Norton, 2010), 122–49.

17   not a muzzle: See Tyler Austin Harper, "I'm a Black Professor. You Don't Need to Bring That Up," *The Atlantic*, August 14, 2023:

Harper describes how antiracist ideology and training has "a troubling, even racist subtext: that white and Black Americans are so radically different that interracial relationships require careful management, constant eggshell-walking, and even expert guidance from professional antiracists. Rather than producing racial harmony, this new ethos frequently has the opposite effect, making white-Black interactions stressful, unpleasant, or, perhaps most often, simply weird."

17 "It's not rocket science": Conversation with author, July 13, 2023.

III. Law after the 1960s: Replacing Institutional Authority with Individual Rights

18 "a massive redefinition of freedom": Eric Foner, *The Story of American Freedom* (New York: W.W. Norton, 1998), 293.

19 "not any particular power": Charles A. Reich, "The New Property," 73 Yale L.J. 733, 774 (1964). Hannah Arendt observed that "the liberal writer is apt to pay little attention" to the "distinction between legitimate and illegitimate power . . . because of his conviction that all power corrupts and that the constancy of progress requires constant loss of power, no matter what its origin may be." Hannah Arendt, "What Is Authority?," in *The Portable Hannah Arendt* (New York: Penguin, 2003), 466.

19 framework of American law was largely rebuilt: See Philip K. Howard, "History of American Law Since 1968," in *Oxford Companion to American Law*, ed. Kermit L. Hall (New York: Oxford University Press, 2002), 392.

19 forest rangers: Herbert Kaufman, *The Forest Ranger: A Study in Administrative Behavior* (Washington, DC: RFF Press, 2006). See introduction by Philip K. Howard to Herbert Kaufman, *Red Tape: Its Origins, Uses, and Abuses* (Washington, DC: Brookings Institution Press, 2015).

19 Safety in the workplace: See discussion in Philip K. Howard, *The Death of Common Sense: How Law Is Suffocating America* (New York: Random House, 1995), 11–22.

20 "fixed route of march": Max Weber, *Economy and Society*, eds. Guenther Roth and Claus Wittich (Berkeley, CA: University of California Press, 1978), 956-1002. See also Frederick Winslow Taylor, *The Principles of Scientific Management* (New York: W.W. Norton, 1967), 6–7: "In the past the man has been first. In the

future the system must be first . . . The best management is a true science, resting upon clearly defined laws, rules, and principles."

20   "Only precise, specific guidelines": Kaufman, *Red Tape*, 31.

20   The "legal process" movement: See Henry Hart and Albert Sacks, *The Legal Process: Basic Problems in the Making and Application of Law* (1958) (unpublished manuscript), lxxxiv.

20   Giving a permit: See, e.g., Philip K. Howard, "Two Years, Not Ten Years: Redesigning Infrastructure Approvals," Common Good, September 2015, and Philip K. Howard, *The Rule of Nobody: Saving America from Dead Laws and Broken Government* (New York: W.W. Norton, 2014), 9–13.

20   disciplining a public employee: See, e.g., Philip K. Howard, *Not Accountable: Rethinking the Constitutionality of Public Employee Unions* (Garden City, NY: Rodin, 2023), 51–57.

21   Almost any ordinary accident: See discussion in Philip K. Howard, *The Collapse of the Common Good: How America's Lawsuit Culture Undermines Our Freedom* (New York: Ballantine, 2001), 3–70, and Philip K. Howard, *Life Without Lawyers: Restoring Responsibility in America* (New York: W.W. Norton, 2010), 15–18, 68–92.

21   "conclusions masquerading as reasons": Cass R. Sunstein, "Rights and Their Critics Propter Honoris Respectum," 70 *Notre Dame Law Review* 727, 742 (1995).

21   "considerations of social advantage": Oliver Wendell Holmes, Jr., "The Path of the Law," 10 *Harvard Law Review* 457, 467–68 (1897).

21   "subject to . . . the calculus of social interests": John Rawls, *A Theory of Justice* (Cambridge, MA: Harvard University Press, 1999), 4.

22   "lost the distinction between right and wrong": Alan Wolfe, *One Nation, After All: What Middle-Class Americans Really Think about God, Country, Family, Racism, Welfare, Immigration, Homosexuality, Work, the Right, the Left, and Each Other* (New York: Viking, 1998), 300.

22   "a form of authoritarianism": P. S. Atiyah, "From Principles to Pragmatism: Changes in the Function of the Judicial Process and the Law," 65 *Iowa Law Review* 1249, 1268 (1980).

23   Sociologist Nathan Glazer: Nathan Glazer, *The Limits of Social Policy* (Cambridge, MA: Harvard University Press, 1988), 1–2. See discussion in Kenneth R. Hammond, *Human Judgment and*

Social Policy: Irreducible Uncertainty, Inevitable Error, Unavoidable Injustice (New York: Oxford University Press, 1996), 190–91.

23 **"crossword puzzle to be solved"**: Václav Havel, *The Art of the Impossible: Politics as Morality in Practice* (New York: Knopf, 1997), 105.

23 **Conflicting interests are unavoidable**: "Liberty for wolves," Isaiah Berlin observed, "is death for the lambs." Isaiah Berlin, *The Crooked Timber of Humanity: Chapters in the History of Ideas* (New York: Knopf, 1991), 12–13.

23 **"the increasing delegitimization of authority"**: Michel J. Crozier, Samuel P. Huntington, and Joji Watanuki, *The Crisis of Democracy: Report on the Governability of Democracies to the Trilateral Commission* (New York: New York University Press, 1975), 162.

IV. The Architecture of Everyday Freedom

24 **"The end of law is not to . . . restrain"**: John Locke, *The Second Treatise on Civil Government* (Amherst, MA: Prometheus, 1986), 33.

25 **Citizens find themselves stymied**: See generally Philip K. Howard, *The Death of Common Sense: How Law Is Suffocating America* (New York: Random House, 1995); Philip K. Howard, *The Collapse of the Common Good: How America's Lawsuit Culture Undermines Our Freedom* (New York: Ballantine, 2001); and Philip K. Howard, *Life Without Lawyers: Restoring Responsibility in America* (New York: W.W. Norton, 2010).

25 **Elected and appointed officials**: See Philip K. Howard, *Not Accountable: Rethinking the Constitutionality of Public Employee Unions* (Garden City, NY: Rodin, 2023), 17–23, 83–94: Philip K. Howard, *The Rule of Nobody: Saving America from Dead Laws and Broken Government* (New York: W.W. Norton, 2014), 14–27.

26 **"It is one of the most prominent features"**: James Madison, speech in Congress on the Removal Power, May 19, 1789, in *Writings* (New York: Library of America: 1999), 435.

26 **"Justice is a concept"**: Benjamin N. Cardozo, *The Growth of the Law* (New Haven, CT: Yale University Press, 1924), 87.

26 **"The task of making a moral decision"**: Hans-Georg Gadamer, *Truth and Method*, trans. Joel Weinsheimer and Donald G. Marshall, 2nd ed. (New York: Continuum, 1998), 317.

26 The letter of the law: See discussion in Howard, *The Rule of Nobody*, 34–43. Aleksandr Solzhenitsyn powerfully makes this point, discussed later.

28 "frontiers, not artificially drawn": Isaiah Berlin, "Two Concepts of Liberty," from *The Proper Study of Mankind: An Anthology of Essays*, eds. Henry Hardy and Roger Hausneer (New York: Farrar, Straus and Giroux, 2000), 236.

28 In these and other ways: Economist Douglass North received the Nobel prize for analysis of how law and other institutional and informal norms create trustworthy frameworks for impersonal exchange. Douglass C. North, "Institutions," 5 J. of Econ. Perspectives 97 (1991). See discussion in Julio Faundez, "Douglass North's Theory of Institutions: Lessons for Law and Development," 8 *Hague Journal on the Rule of Law* 373 (2016).

30 "the first requirement": Oliver Wendell Holmes, Jr., *The Common Law* (Clark, NJ: Lawbook Exchange, 2005), 41.

30 Principles are far superior: See discussion in Howard, *The Rule of Nobody*, 63–74.

30 In the 1980s, Australia: John Braithwaite and Valerie Braithwaite, "The Politics of Legalism: Rules Versus Standards in Nursing-Home Regulation," 4 *Social & Legal Studies* 307, 310–26 (1995). See discussion in Howard, *The Rule of Nobody*, 47–49.

31 "standards that capture lay intuitions": Richard A. Posner, *The Problems of Jurisprudence*, (Cambridge, MA: Harvard University Press, 1990), 48. See discussion in Howard, *The Death of Common Sense*, 176–81.

31 "mightily addicted to rules": David Hume, *A Treatise of Human Nature*, eds. L. A. Selby-Bigge and P. H. Nidditch (Oxford: Oxford University Press, 1978), 551.

32 distance learning: See, e.g., Frederick M. Hess and Hayley Boling, "Are Teachers Unions Overplaying Their Hands?," *The Dispatch*, July 31, 2020.

32 "to cover every case": John Dewey, "Logical Method and Law," 10 *Cornell Law Review* 17 (1924), 26.

32 The uncertainty inherent in principles-based law: See discussion in Howard, *The Rule of Nobody*, 63–74.

32 "like the hole in a doughnut": Ronald M. Dworkin, *Taking Rights Seriously* (Cambridge, MA: Harvard University Press, 1978), 31.

32 "The Optimum Precision of Administrative Rules": Colin S. Diver, "The Optimal Precision of Administrative Rules," 93 *Yale Law Journal* 65 (November 1983).

33 Management professor Brenda Zimmerman: Brenda Zimmerman, as quoted in David Segal, "It's Complicated: Making Sense of Complexity," *The New York Times*, May 1, 2010. See also Frances Westley, Brenda Zimmerman, and Michael Patton, *Getting to Maybe: How the World Is Changed* (Toronto: Vintage, 2007).

34 If teachers: See Richard Arum, *Judging School Discipline: The Crisis of Moral Authority* (Cambridge, MA: Harvard University Press, 2005).

34 If supervisors: See discussion in Howard, *Life Without Lawyers*, 122–49.

35 If inspectors: See discussion in Howard, *The Death of Common Sense*, 11–15, and Howard, *The Rule of Nobody*, 36–38.

35 If hospital administrators: See, e.g., Amanda J. Moy, et al., "Measurement of Clinical Documentation Burden Among Physicians and Nurses Using Electronic Health Records: A Scoping Review," 28 *Journal of the American Medical Informatics Association* 998 (2021).

35 If university presidents and deans: See, e.g., Kate McGee and James Barragán, "Texas A&M Suspended Professor Accused of Criticizing Lt. Gov. Dan Patrick in Lecture," *The Texas Tribune*, July 25, 2023, and Ruth Marcus, "Stanford Students Lost a Chance to Learn When They Shouted Down a Judge," *The Wall Street Journal*, March 27, 2023.

35 Take away the authority of people with responsibility: See Hannah Arendt, "What Is Authority?," in *The Portable Hannah Arendt* (New York: Penguin, 2003), 469, discussing how the "simultaneous recession of both freedom and authority" is not a coincidence. See discussion in Howard, *The Collapse of the Common Good*, 144–55.

V. It's OK to Walk Away: The Flawed Assumptions of Current Law that Cause Failure and Alienation

37 "When you strike at a king": Sheldon M. Novick, Letter, "What Emerson Said," *The New York Times*, October 15, 1989, 58.

37   "Government in all its actions": Friedrich A. Hayek, *The Road to Serfdom*, ed. Bruce Caldwell (Chicago: University of Chicago Press, 2007), 112.

37   "Let all the laws be clear, uniform, and precise": Voltaire, as quoted in John R. Howe, *Language and Political Meaning in Revolutionary America* (Amherst: University of Massachusetts Press, 2004), 38.

38   "Words do not determine meaning": Jeremy Waldron, "Vagueness in Law and Language: Some Philosophical Issues," 82 *California Law Review* 509, 510 (1994).

38   "the world, like a kaleidoscope": Michael Polanyi, *Personal Knowledge: Towards a Post-Critical Philosophy* (Chicago: University of Chicago Press, 1962), 79.

38   "A result arrived at": Polanyi, *Personal Knowledge*, 311.

39   About 150 million words: See Philip K. Howard, "A Radical Centrist Platform for 2020," *The Hill*, April 13, 2019.

39   "cognitive overload": See discussion of the work of psychologist John Sweller in Philip K. Howard, "Bureaucracy vs. Democracy," *The American Interest*, January 31, 2019, and a more extensive discussion in "Bureaucracy vs. Democracy: Examining the Bureaucratic Causes of Public Failure, Economic Repression, and Voter Alienation," Columbia University Center on Capitalism and Society, Working Paper No. 113, February 4, 2019. See also Barry Schwartz and Kenneth Sharpe, *Practical Wisdom: The Right Way to Do the Right Thing* (New York: Riverhead, 2010), 41–42 (increasing checklists for firefighters increased confusion and reduced survival rates).

39   In their study of Illinois nursing home regulation: John Braithwaite and Valerie Braithwaite, *The Politics of Legalism: Rules Versus Standards in Nursing-Home Regulation*, 4 *Social & Legal Studies* 307 (1995).

39   "It will be of little avail": James Madison, "Federalist No. 62," in Alexander Hamilton, John Jay, and James Madison, *The Federalist Papers* (Project Gutenberg eBook, 1998).

40   To instill trust in personnel decisions: See, e.g., Jeffrey Liker and Michael Hoseus, *Toyota Culture: The Heart and Soul of the Toyota Way* (New York: McGraw-Hill, 2008), 414–18.

40   public input: As a young lawyer, I was chair of the zoning committee of Manhattan Community Board 6, and presided over

public hearings for zoning applications, after which we would provide public input to the City Planning Commission. I found comments from the public, on balance, added a perspective that could be useful to decision-makers.

40 *The Moral Life of Schools*: Philip W. Jackson, Robert E. Boostrom, and David T. Hansen, *The Moral Life of Schools* (San Francisco: Jossey-Bass, 1998), 48: "What we reject about the words *objective* and *subjective* is the implication that one refers to something real and the other does not."

40 **"We had a teacher here"**: Author interview with Ryan Hill, 2008. See discussion in Philip K. Howard, *Life Without Lawyers: Restoring Responsibility in America* (New York: W.W. Norton, 2010), 122–49.

41 **"Two Years, Not Ten Years"**: Philip K. Howard, "Two Years, Not Ten Years: Redesigning Infrastructure Approvals,"

42 **Building new transmission lines:** See, e.g., Robinson Meyer, "Manchin's New Bill Could Lead to One Big Climate Win," *The Atlantic*, September 21, 2022.

42 **There's near-zero accountability:** See discussion in Philip K. Howard, *Not Accountable: Rethinking the Constitutionality of Public Employee Unions* (Garden City, NY: Rodin, 2023), 51–57.

42 **Over an eighteen-year study period in Illinois:** Terry Moe, *Special Interest: Teachers Unions and America's Public Schools* (Washington, DC: Brookings Institution Press, 2011), 186.

42 **Over 99 percent of federal employees:** Memorandum from Robert Goldenkoff, director of strategic issues, U.S. Government Accountability Office, to Ron Johnson, chairman, Senate Committee on Homeland Security and Governmental Affairs (May 9, 2016), 5.

42 **Because teachers and school administrators:** Richard Arum, *Judging School Discipline: The Crisis of Moral Authority* (Cambridge, MA: Harvard University Press, 2005), 169.

43 **Because procedures designed to assure a fair trial:** William J. Stuntz, *The Collapse of American Criminal Justice* (Cambridge, MA: Harvard University Press, 2011), 39, 302.

43 **"we can't afford to keep winning cases"**: Recounted to the author by a lawyer for the CEO.

43 **Requiring cops to demonstrate probable cause:** See, e.g., Christopher Slobogin, "Testilying: Police Perjury and What to Do about It," 67 *University of Colorado Law Review* 1037 (1996).

43 **"insistence on after-the-fact justification":** Gerd Gigerenzer, *Gut Feelings: The Intelligence of the Unconscious* (New York: Penguin, 2008), 15.

44 **"Objectivism has totally falsified":** Polanyi, *Personal Knowledge*, 286.

45 **A Public Agenda survey:** Public Agenda, "Teaching Interrupted: Do Discipline Policies in Today's Public Schools Foster the Common Good?," May 2004, 2–3.

45 **College students regularly assert:** See, e.g., Jeannie Suk Gersen, "What If Trigger Warnings Don't Work?" *The New Yorker*, September 28, 2021. See Jill Filipovic, "I Was Wrong About Trigger Warnings," *The Atlantic*, August 9, 2023.

45 **employers don't provide candid feedback:** See discussion in Philip K. Howard, *The Collapse of the Common Good: How America's Lawsuit Culture Undermines Our Freedom* (New York: Ballantine, 2001) 181–86, and Howard, *Life Without Lawyers*, 142–45.

45 **college professors and students:** See, e.g., Jocelyn Gecker, "A College in Upheaval: War on 'Woke' Sparks Fear in Florida," Associated Press, March 30, 2023.

45 **Government became largely unmanageable:** See generally Daniel DiSalvo, *Government against Itself: Public Union Power and Its Consequences* (New York: Oxford University Press, 2015) and Howard, *Not Accountable*.

46 **This requires that judges:** Philip K. Howard, "Making Civil Justice Sane," *City Journal*, Spring 2006.

46 **Teachers no longer will hug a crying child:** See, e.g., Linda Borg, "Teachers Afraid to Hug Pupils," *The Providence Journal*, December 2, 2017.

46 **Hospitals and doctors practice defensive medicine:** See, e.g., Chad Terhune, "The $200 Billion Perils of Unnecessary Medical Tests," PBS NewsHour, May 24, 2017. See also Philip K. Howard, "Just Medicine," *The New York Times*, April 1, 2009.

46 **Parents impede the emotional growth of children:** See, e.g., Nicole B. Perry, et al., "Childhood Self-Regulation as a

Mechanism Through Which Early Overcontrolling Parenting Is Associated with Adjustment in Preadolescence," 54 *Developmental Psychology* 1542 (2018) (finding that overcontrolling parenting in early childhood is associated with reduced emotional regulation and inhibitory control in early adolescence), and Lenore Skenazy, "Helicopter Parents Need To Stop Treating Kids like Luxury Tourists," *New York Post,* March 3, 2022 (arguing that increasingly restrictive "helicopter parenting" increases anxiety and reduces independence in children).

47 **"Negligence . . . [is] a standard of conduct":** Oliver Wendell Holmes, Jr., "Law in Science and Science in Law," 12 *Harvard Law Review* 443, 458 (1899).

48 **"An act is illegal":** Donald J. Black, "The Mobilization of Law," 2 *The Journal of Legal Studies* 125, 131 n. 24 (1973).

48 **In a famous 2003 case:** *Tomlinson v. Congleton Borough Council* [2004] 1 AC 46.

49 **"What is the object of a jury trial?":** Bernard Bailyn, ed., *The Debate on the Constitution: Federalist and Antifederalist Speeches, Articles, and Letters During the Struggle over Ratification, Part Two: January to August 1788* (New York: Library of America, 1993), 736.

49 **In one crazy case:** See discussion Howard, *Life Without Lawyers,* 72–73.

49 **RAND Corporation found that 90 percent of claimants:** Stephen J. Carroll, et al., "Asbestos Litigation Costs, Compensation, and Alternatives," RAND Research Brief (2005).

50 **"basic moral principle":** Eugene V. Rostow, "American Legal Realism and the Sense of the Profession," 34 *Rocky Mountain Law Review* 123, 126 (1962).

51 **"Laws on paper are meaningless":** Lawrence M. Friedman, "Legal Rules and the Process of Social Change," 19 *Stanford Law Review* 786, 790 (April 1967).

VI. Rebuilding Trust for a Flourishing Society

53 **The Importance of Trust:** In her Reith Lectures, philosopher Onora O'Neill recounts that "Confucius told his disciple Tzu-kung that three things are needed for government: weapons, food and trust. If a ruler can't hold on to all three, he should give up the weapons first and the food next. Trust should be guarded to the end: without trust we cannot stand." Onora O'Neill, *A Question of Trust: The BBC Reith Lectures 2002* (Cambridge, UK: Cambridge University Press, 2002), 3.

53   "Trust and similar values": Kenneth J. Arrow, *The Limits of Organization* (New York: Oxford University Press, 1974), 23.

54   Tim Carney: Timothy P. Carney, *Alienated America: Why Some Places Thrive While Others Collapse* (New York: HarperCollins, 2019), 259-280.

54   "conform voluntarily to certain principles": Friedrich A. Hayek, *The Constitution of Liberty*, ed. Ronald Hamowy (Chicago: University of Chicago Press, 2011), 123.

54   "The most important principle": Jonathan Haidt, *The Righteous Mind: Why Good People Are Divided by Politics and Religion* (New York: Vintage, 2013), 86.

54   In administering price controls: Ian Ayres and John Braithwaite, *Responsive Regulation: Transcending the Deregulation Debate* (New York: Oxford University Press, 1992), 26.

55   a culture of defensiveness: Distrust of justice is why employers don't feel free to give job references or provide candid reviews; why parents must sign liability waivers for field trips and other children's activities; why companies plaster warning labels on almost every product: "Caution, Contents Are Hot." See discussion in Philip K. Howard, *The Collapse of the Common Good: How America's Lawsuit Culture Undermines Our Freedom* (New York: Ballantine, 2001), 3–70.

55   Asked if they would trust justice: Regina Corso and Elizabeth Shores, "Public Trust of Civil Justice," Harris Interactive, June 20, 2005, 8.

55   preoccupied with avoiding error: Onora O'Neill talks about distrust of institutional choices partially as a function of too much accountability: "Plants don't flourish when we pull them up too often to check the roots." *A Question of Trust*, 19. But distrust of authority is far more corrosive than too much accountability, because, as discussed earlier, the judgments needed are usually not susceptible to objective accountability. The distrust of authority warps institutional choices towards what is provable instead of what's right or sensible.

55   Revert towards self-interest: David Brooks, "How America Got Mean," *The Atlantic*, August 14, 2023.

55 **"culture of resistance":** Joel F. Handler, *Law and the Search for Community* (New Orleans: Quid Pro, 2010), 35. Tocqueville similarly observed that resistance sets in when people are given detailed dictates such as "'you shall act just as I please' . . . These are not the conditions on which the alliance of the human will is to be obtained; it must be free in its gait and responsible for its acts." Alexis de Tocqueville, *Democracy in America*, ed. Phillips Bradley (New York: Vintage, 1990), 1: 90.

55 **stilted language of political correctness:** Sociologist Orlando Patterson observed that "No Euro-American person, except one insensitive to the charge of racism, dares say what he or she really means." Orlando Patterson, *The Ordeal of Integration:* Progress and Resentment in America's "Racial" Crisis (New York: Basic Civitas, 1997), 2. See Tyler Austin Harper, "I'm a Black Professor. You Don't Need to Bring That Up," *The Atlantic*, August 14, 2023. As I discuss in *The Collapse of the Common Good*, Black-white relations in the workplace suffer from this distrust spiral as lack of candor leads to suspicions of prejudice. Howard, *The Collapse of the Common Good*, 173–98.

55 **Building trust is impossible:** See O'Neill, *A Question of Trust*, 72–73. Polanyi makes a similar point: The "network of mutual trust, on which the factual consensus of a free society depends, is fragile. Any conflict which sharply divides people will tend to destroy their mutual trust and make universal agreement on the facts bearing on the conflict difficult to achieve." Michael Polanyi, *Personal Knowledge: Towards a Post-Critical Philosophy* (Chicago: University of Chicago Press, 1962), 241.

56 **"the sense by which we take our bearings":** Hannah Arendt, "Truth and Politics," in *The Portable Hannah Arendt* (New York: Penguin, 2003), 568.

56 **"deny the evidence of your senses":** George Orwell, *1984* (Berkeley, CA: University Press Books, 2017), 71: "The Party told you to reject the evidence of your eyes and ears. It was their final, most essential command."

56 **Distrust discourages constructive behavior:** When an Israeli school levied fines to try to discourage late pickups by parents at the end of the day, tardiness increased. Late pickups decreased when picking up children on time became a moral obligation. See Barry Schwartz and Kenneth Sharpe, *Practical Wisdom: The Right Way to Do the Right Thing* (New York: Riverhead, 2010), 190–92.

56 **"The de-skilling of teachers":** Schwartz and Sharpe, *Practical Wisdom*, 174–76.

57 **"vetocracy":** Francis Fukuyama, *Political Order and Political Decay: From the Industrial Revolution to the Globalization of Democracy* (New York: Farrar, Straus and Giroux, 2014), 488.

57 *The Moral Basis of a Backward Society*: Edward C. Banfield, *The Moral Basis of a Backward Society* (New York: Free Press, 1958), 92, 120.

58 *Alienated America*: Carney, *Alienated America*, 203–36.

58 **"extreme partisanship may be literally addictive":** Jonathan Haidt, *The Righteous Mind: Why Good People Are Divided by Politics and Religion* (New York: Vintage, 2013), 103.

58 **Jonah Goldberg:** Jonah Goldberg, "When Reality Is a Punch in the Face," *The Dispatch*, July 7, 2023. Astronomer Harlow Shapley in the 1950s listed five events that could destroy the earth, including boredom. He also feared a "maniac genius" and a plague. See discussion in Robert Nisbet, *Twilight of Authority* (Indianapolis: Liberty Fund, 1975), 86.

59 **I-95 in Philadelphia Repair:** See Gregory Korte, Mark Niquette, and Skylar Woodhouse, "How the I-95 Bridge Reopened Just 12 Days after Fiery Collapse," *Bloomberg*, June 28, 2023; Aidan Mackenzie, "Can I-95's Repairs Teach Us to Build Faster?," Institute for Progress, July 7, 2023; William D. Eggers and Donald F. Kettl, "Government Can't Be Agile? Don't Tell Pennsylvania's Bridge-Fixers," Governing, August 8, 2023; and Jake Blumgart, "The Battle for I-95," *The Atlantic*, June 26, 2023.

60 **Public contracting procedures:** See, e.g., Citizens Budget Commission, "9 Things New Yorkers Should Know about How New York City Buys Stuff," February 21, 2019 (finding that the "lengthy, convoluted" process of contracting and procurement in NYC generates significant additional costs). See discussion in Philip K. Howard, *The Death of Common Sense: How Law Is Suffocating America* (New York: Random House, 1995), 66–76.

60 **Permits can take years:** See generally Philip K. Howard, "Two Years, Not Ten Years: Redesigning Infrastructure Approvals," Common Good, September 2015. See also Ezra Klein, "The Problem with Everything-Bagel Liberalism," *The New York Times*, April 2, 2023.

61 **Studies on public corruption:** See, e.g., Frank Anechiarico and James B. Jacobs, *The Pursuit of Absolute Integrity: How Corruption Control Makes Government Ineffective* (Chicago: University of Chicago Press, 1996); State-City Commission on Integrity in Government (the Sovern Commission), "Report and Recommendations Relating to City Procurement and Contracts," November 19, 1986.

61 **"The sole and undivided responsibility":** Alexander Hamilton, "Federalist No. 76," in Alexander Hamilton, John Jay, and James Madison, *The Federalist Papers* (Project Gutenberg eBook, 1998).

61 **"shifted from one to another":** Alexander Hamilton, "Federalist No. 70," in Alexander Hamilton, John Jay, and James Madison, *The Federalist Papers* (Project Gutenberg eBook, 1998). George Washington made a similar point: "Whenever one person is found adequate to the discharge of a duty . . . it is worse executed by two persons, and scarcely done at all if three or more are employed." Leonard D. White, *The Federalists: A Study in Administrative History* (New York: Macmillan, 1948), 91.

61 **Ditto with "Operation Warp Speed":** See generally U.S. Government Accountability Office, "Operation Warp Speed: Accelerated COVID-19 Vaccine Development Status and Efforts to Address Manufacturing Challenges," February 2021.

61 **In 2023, Baltimore found that in twenty-three public schools:** Chris Papst, "23 Baltimore Schools Have Zero Students Proficient in Math, per State Test Results," Fox45News, February 6, 2023.

61 **In Chicago, thirty-seven schools:** Ted Dabrowski and John Klingler, "Not a Single Student Can Do Math at Grade Level in 53 Illinois Schools. For Reading, It's 30 Schools," WirePoints, February 14, 2023.

62 **"there have to be people who make decisions":** Peter F. Drucker, *Post-Capitalist Society* (New York: HarperCollins, 1994), 56.

63 **"Choosing among values":** Charles E. Wyzanski, Jr., "Equal Justice Through Law," 47 *Tulane Law Review* 951, 959 (1973).

63 **Such as when a toddler:** See discussion in Philip K. Howard, *The Rule of Nobody: Saving America from Dead Laws and Broken Government* (New York: W.W. Norton, 2014), 51.

63 **Government procurement rules:** Howard, *The Death of Common Sense*, 166–76.

64 Like a kind of black magic: People can argue almost any-thing—such as the plaintiff in the ridiculous $54 million lost pants lawsuit who argued that "no case . . . comes anywhere close to [this] outrageousness." See discussion in Howard, *Life Without Lawyers*, 72–73. It's easy to make a claim that something that might have been done differently. Why didn't the hospital do that one extra test? Why didn't the supervisor authorize extra training before letting the employee go?

64 "The spirit of distrust of authority": Robert Kagan, "Adversarial Legalism and American Government," 10 *Journal of Policy Analysis & Management* 369, 375 (1991).

64 "at least to be open to the possibility": Michael Lipsky, *Street-Level Bureaucracy: Dilemmas of the Individual in Public Services* (New York: Russell Sage, 1980), 161. Some jurisdictions, for exam-ple, allow deviation from rules as long the exceptions are approved and transparent. See Kathleen G. Noonan, Charles F. Sabel, and William H. Simon, "Legal Accountability in the Service-Based Welfare State: Lessons from Child Welfare Reform," 34 *Law & Social Inquiry* 523, 537–38 (Summer 2009): Central administration gives "frontline offices and workers . . . relatively broad discretion to apply governing principles," Professors Noonan, Sabel, and Simon report, allowing it to "monitor [their] success in achieving the goals" and "learn from local practice while correcting its mistakes." See discussion in Howard, *The Rule of Nobody*, 49–52.

64 "domain of human action": John Fletcher Moulton, "Law and Manners," *The Atlantic*, July 1942.

65 David Brooks: David Brooks, "How America Got Mean," *The Atlantic*, August 14, 2023.

65 "is too cold and formal": Aleksandr Solzhenitsyn, *Solzhenitsyn at Harvard: The Address, Twelve Early Responses, and Six Later Reflections*, ed. Ronald Berman (Washington, DC: Ethics and Public Policy Center, 1980), 8, 14. Solzhenitsyn saw growing legalisms leading Americans away from core values of self-determination: "A society based on the letter of the law and never reaching any higher fails to take advantage of the full range of human possibilities. The letter of the law is too cold and formal to have a beneficial influence on society. Whenever the tissue of life is woven of legalistic relation-ships, this creates an atmosphere of spiritual mediocrity that para-lyzes man's noblest impulses . . . After a certain level of the problem has been reached, legalistic thinking induces paralysis; it prevents one from seeing the scale and the meaning of events."

65 **"the interpreter for the community"**: Benjamin N. Cardozo, *The Nature of the Judicial Process* (New Haven, CT: Yale University Press, 1921), 16.

VII. Institutional Authority Is Vital to Everyday Freedom

67 **An institution provides the purpose**: See, e.g., Larry M. Preston, *Freedom and the Organizational Republic* (New York: De Gruyer, 1991), 138: "Our freedom depends at least as much on the character of life within institutions as on the principles" of government. Historian Eric Foner says what John Dewey called "effective freedom" meant "the ability to shape the institutions that determine the lineaments of freedom." Eric Foner, *The Story of American Freedom* (New York: W.W. Norton, 1998), xvii.

67 **institutions empower people**: See discussion in Philip K. Howard, *Try Common Sense: Replacing the Failed Ideologies of Right and Left* (New York: W.W. Norton, 2019), 87–89.

67 **Ideas accelerate, economist Paul Romer found**: See, e.g., Paul M. Romer, "Endogenous Technological Change," 98 *Journal of Political Economy* S71 (1990).

68 **An entire industry for morality training**: Compulsory training protocols are now universal among institutions.

68 **Professors are afraid to continue conversations**: Personal experience of the author.

68 **Practical Wisdom**: Barry Schwartz and Kenneth Sharpe, *Practical Wisdom: The Right Way to Do the Right Thing* (New York: Riverhead, 2010), 13–17.

69 **It makes a huge difference**: Amy Wrzesniewski, "Finding Positive Meaning in Work," in *Positive Organizational Scholarship: Foundations of a New Discipline*, eds. Kim S. Cameron, Jane E. Dutton, and Robert E. Quinn (San Francisco: Berrett-Koehler, 2003).

69 **The human qualities that instill purpose**: Too much emphasis on incentives and metrics, as Jerry Z. Müller describes in *The Tyranny of Metrics*, undermines the many subtle values needed for long term success. Jerry Z. Müller, *The Tyranny of Metrics* (Princeton: Princeton University Press, 2018). Metrics often cause failure. For example, "surgical report cards"—aimed at identifying surgeons with fewest adverse outcomes—have the paradoxical effect of driving the best surgeons away from the hard cases where they are needed most. (Sandeep Jauhar, M.D., "The Pitfalls of Linking Doctors' Pay to Performance," *The New York Times*, September 8, 2008.) Evaluating teachers by test scores transforms schools into drill sheds, without joy or curiosity. (See, e.g., Anya Kamenetz, *The Test: Why Our Schools Are Obsessed with Standardized Testing—But You Don't Have to Be* (New York: Public Affairs, 2015).) Paying bankers for new accounts at Wells Fargo Bank led to a scandal of phony accounts, destroying a material percentage of the bank's value. (John Foley, "Wells Fargo Labors under $100 Bln in Sin Discount," Reuters, January 10, 2023). However powerful artificial intelligence becomes, it is unlikely to make personnel decisions that people will trust.

69 **"character traits like loyalty"**: Schwartz and Sharpe, *Practical Wisdom*, 6.

69 **"the most important thing"**: Philip W. Jackson, Robert E. Boostrom, and David T. Hansen, *The Moral Life of Schools* (San Francisco: Jossey-Bass, 1998), 115.

69 **"a readiness to perceive and act"**: Michael Polanyi, *Personal Knowledge: Towards a Post-Critical Philosophy* (Chicago: University of Chicago Press, 1962), 120.

69 **"We note deep disaffection"**: The National Commission on Public Service, "Urgent Business for America: Revitalizing the Federal Government for the 21st Century," January 2003, 12.

70 **"Laying aside all exceptions to the rule"**: Jackson, Boostrom, and Hansen, *The Moral Life of Schools*, 34. Emerson made a similar point. People "imagine that they communicate their virtue or vice only by overt actions and do not see that virtue or vice emit a breath every moment . . . We pass for what we are." Ralph Waldo Emerson, "Self-Reliance," in *Ralph Waldo Emerson: The Major Prose*, eds. Ronald A. Bosco and Joel Myerson (Cambridge, MA: Harvard University Press, 2015), 134. Polanyi describes the cumulative nature of judgments about people: "For men are valued as men according to their moral force; and the outcome . . . is assessed, not as the success or failure of any external performance of ours, but by its effect on our whole person." Polanyi, *Personal Knowledge*, 215.

70 **"much longer and more leisurely"**: Jonathan Haidt, "The Emotional Dog and Its Rational Tail: A Social Intuitionist Approach to Moral Judgment," 108 *Psychological Review* 814, 820 (2001).

70 **"Eleventh Commandment"**: Alan Wolfe, *One Nation, After All: What Middle-Class Americans Really Think about God, Country, Family, Racism, Welfare, Immigration, Homosexuality, Work, the Right, the Left, and Each Other* (New York: Viking, 1998), 54. See also Hannah Arendt, "Banality and Conscience," in *The Portable Hannah Arendt* (New York: Penguin, 2003), 386: "About nothing does public opinion everywhere seem to be in happier agreement than that no one has the right to judge somebody else."

71 **worker councils**: See, e.g., Jeffrey Liker and Michael Hoseus, *Toyota Culture: The Heart and Soul of the Toyota Way* (New York: McGraw-Hill, 2008), 414–18.

71 **But this argument is obviously circular**: See Mary Ann Glendon, *Rights Talk: The Impoverishment of Political Discourse* (New York: Free Press, 1991).

71 **"boundless variety of human nature"**: Friedrich A. Hayek, *The Constitution of Liberty*, ed. Ronald Hamowy (Chicago: University of Chicago Press, 2011), 149.

71 **The "unlikeness" of every person**: Hannah Arendt, *Responsibility and Judgment* (New York: Schocken, 2003), 208.

71 **"neither good nor bad"**: Chester Irving Barnard, *The Functions of the Executive* (Cambridge, MA: Harvard University Press, 1968), 218.

72 **It would be far preferable**: See, e.g., Ida Auken, "Danes Don't Have a Minimum Wage. We Have Something Even Better," *The Washington Post*, March 8, 2021.

72 **Trust within institutions can fail for many reasons**: See, e.g., David Brooks, "America Is Having a Moral Convulsion," *The Atlantic*, October 5, 2020.

72 **to prevent judgments on accountability**: See discussion in Philip K. Howard, *Not Accountable: Rethinking the Constitutionality of Public Employee Unions* (Garden City, NY: Rodin, 2023), 51–57.

VIII. Community Responsibility and Social Cohesion

73 **"the art of associating together"**: Alexis de Tocqueville, *Democracy in America*, ed. Phillips Bradley (New York: Vintage, 1990), 2:110.

73 **Community activities keep people's feet on the ground**: Tocqueville, *Democracy in America*, 1:68: "The native of New

England is attached to his township . . . his cooperation in its affairs ensures his attachment to its interests; the well-being it affords him secures his affection; and its welfare is the aim of his ambition and of his future exertions . . . He acquires a taste for order, comprehends the balance of powers, and collects clear practical notions on the nature of his duties and the extent of his rights." Václav Havel similarly saw community activity as a salve to social resentment: "A modern democratic state . . . must offer citizens a colorful array of ways to become involved, both privately and publicly, and must develop very different types of civic coexistence, solidarity, and participation . . . A genuine civil society is, moreover, the best insurance against various kinds of social tension and political or social upheavals; it makes it possible for various problems to be solved immediately, when and where they arise, before they turn septic somewhere under the skin of society." Václav Havel, *The Art of the Impossible: Politics as Morality in Practice* (New York: Knopf, 1997), 147–48.

73 **"norms of reciprocity and trustworthiness":** Robert D. Putnam, *Bowling Alone: The Collapse and Revival of American Community* (New York: Simon & Schuster, 2001), 18–19.

73 **When dealing with concrete situations:** See Stewart Asquith, *Children and Justice: Decision-making in Children's Hearings and Juvenile Courts* (Edinburgh: Edinburgh University Press, 1983). See also M. P. Baumgartner, "The Myth of Discretion," in *The Uses of Discretion*, ed. Keith Hawkins, Oxford Socio-Legal Studies (Oxford: Clarendon, 1992), 129: Leaving aside a few hot-button issues, American judges of different ideological bent generally rule in ways that are "remarkably patterned and consistent."

74 **"point of civil society":** Zack Stanton, "How the 'Culture War' Could Break Democracy," *Politico Magazine*, May 20, 2021 (interview with James Davison Hunter).

74 **The appalling regularity of shootings:** See, e.g., Melanie Warner, "Two Professors Found What Creates a Mass Shooter. Will Politicians Pay Attention?," *Politico Magazine*, May 27, 2022 (interview with Professors Jillian Peterson and James Densley whose profiles of mass shooters find "hopelessness, despair, isolation, self-loathing, oftentimes rejection from peers").

74 **The decline of community after the 1960s:** Putnam, *Bowling Alone*.

74   for example, banning home-cooked meals: See, e.g., William McGurn, "Government vs. Soup Kitchen," *The Wall Street Journal*, November 22, 2011.

74   Mother Teresa abandoned plans: Sam Roberts, "Fight City Hall? Nope, Not Even Mother Teresa," *The New York Times*, September 17, 1990, B1. See discussion in Philip K. Howard, *The Death of Common Sense: How Law Is Suffocating America* (New York: Random House, 1995), 3–5.

75   for example, resulting in cancelling a Little League game: See, e.g., George Gmelch, "Spring, and a Miss," *The New York Times*, April 29, 1998, A25.

75   What put community on life support: See generally Yuval Levin, *The Fractured Republic: Renewing America's Social Contract in the Age of Individualism* (New York: Basic Books, 2017), Kindle locations 615–16, 873, 3085–86.

75   churches lost membership: See Jim Davis and Michael Graham, *The Great Dechurching: Who's Leaving, Why Are They Going, and What Will It Take to Bring Them Back?* (Grand Rapids, MI: Zondervan, 2023) (churches have lost membership, they conclude, in part because they no longer offer the commitment and dignity of serving others). See also Jake Meador, "The Misunderstood Reason Millions of Americans Stopped Going to Church," *The Atlantic*, July 29, 2023.

75   The effect, as social philosopher Yuval Levin describes: See generally Levin, *The Fractured Republic*. Patrick Deneen similarly has analyzed the bifurcation of American culture between "the liberated individual and the controlling state." Patrick J. Deneen, *Why Liberalism Failed* (New Haven, CT: Yale University Press, 2018), 38.

75   "an American were condemned": Tocqueville, *Democracy in America*, 1:250.

76   "right to be left alone": Robert N. Bellah, et al., *The Good Society* (New York: Vintage, 1992), 9.

76   "human beings as rights-bearing individuals": Matthew Rose, *A World after Liberalism: Philosophers of the Radical Right* (New Haven, CT: Yale University Press, 2021), 154. Oliver Wendell Holmes, Jr., made a similar point: "the rule of joy and the law of duty seem to me all one." Oliver Wendell Holmes, Jr., *The Essential Holmes* (Chicago: University of Chicago Press, 2012), 79.

77   "mindless application of harsh rules": Joel F. Handler,

"Continuing Relationships and the Administrative Process: Social Welfare," 1985 Wisconsin Law Review 687, 702 (1985).

77 **The path back to community leadership:** Appeals for more community responsibility often embrace the principle of "subsidiarity," which would allocate responsibility where possible to local institutions. See discussion in Howard, *The Rule of Nobody*, 94–96, and detailed notes thereto.

77 **Giving communities "power and independence":** Tocqueville, *Democracy in America*, 1:67: "without power and independence a town may contain good subjects, but it can have no active citizens." In my interactions with Amitai Etzioni, Benjamin Barber, and other leaders of the communitarian movement, I could never discern a theory of authority that would spark broad interest and make local ownership of social services a reality.

77 **Giving local organizations:** See Tocqueville, *Democracy in America*, 1:86–97; Brink Lindsey, "What Are Humans For?," The Permanent Problem (Substack), August 1, 2023: Humans are "social creatures with profound . . . needs for interpersonal intimacy and group belonging" with an "unmatched ability to cooperate with each other to achieve common goals."

78 **The Ukrainian mobilization:** Conversation with author, July 18, 2023. Professor Murtazashvili also discussed Ukranian decentralization during "Re-empowering Human Agency," a forum co-hosted by Columbia University's Center on Capitalism and Society and Common Good, April 19, 2023.

79 **"There's no such thing as cancel culture":** Lunch speech attended by the author.

79 **"lost to [our] senses":** Tocqueville, *Democracy in America*, 1:243.

IX. The Freedom to Save Ourselves

80 **"an objective way out of the crisis of objectivism":** Václav Havel, *The Art of the Impossible: Politics as Morality in Practice* (New York: Knopf, 1997), 91.

80 **That's what taking responsibility means:** Friedrich A. Hayek, *The Constitution of Liberty*, ed. Ronald Hamowy (Chicago: University of Chicago Press, 2011), 146: "the essential condition of responsibility is that it refer to circumstances that the individual can judge [and] to problems . . . whose solution he can . . . consider his own."

81 aspiring to a better world: Michael Polanyi, *Personal Knowledge: Towards a Post-Critical Philosophy* (Chicago: University of Chicago Press, 1962), 380: "For human greatness . . . belongs to the family of things which exist only to those committed to them. All manner of excellence . . . can be defined by our respect for human greatness."

81 We don't bail out: Polanyi discusses the human blindness for facts inconsistent with our preconceptions of how things work. On Darwin's voyage, native Fuegians were fascinated by small boats but seemed not to comprehend a ship the size of the *Beagle*. Polanyi, *Personal Knowledge*, 291.

81 proof of our moral probity: The modern quest to avoid asserting beliefs of right and wrong is one of Polanyi's central themes. See Polanyi, *Personal Knowledge*, 271: We have come to believe that "to refrain from belief is always an act of moral probity;" intellectuals have a "yearning for objective standards safe against self doubt" (227); "Objectivism seeks to relieve us of all responsibility for the holding of our beliefs" (323). Havel similarly observed that "We learned not to believe in anything." Havel, *The Art of the Impossible*, 4. In *Eichmann in Jerusalem*, Hannah Arendt writes: "One of the central moral questions of all time . . . [is] the nature and function of human judgment. What we demand is that human beings be capable of telling right from wrong even when all they have to guide them is their own judgment." Hannah Arendt, in *The Portable Hannah Arendt* (New York: Penguin, 2003), 385.

81 "designated by Providence": George Washington, Circular to the States, June 8, 1783, Founders Online (U.S. National Archives).

81 "'to make the best of themselves'": Isaiah Berlin, *Four Essays on Liberty* (Oxford: Oxford University Press, 1969), xlix, quoting Thomas Hill Green.

82 "a free society rests": Peter F. Drucker, *The Age of Discontinuity: Guidelines to Our Changing Society,* 2nd ed. (New Brunswick, N.J.: Transaction, 1992), 37.

82 frozen bureaucratic dictates: Organizational theorist and Nobel laureate Herbert A. Simon criticized bureaucratic requirements as "frozen decisions." Herbert Simon, "Decision-Making and Organizational Design," in *Organizational Theory: Selected Readings*, ed. D. S. Pugh (Baltimore: Penguin, 1971), 189–212.

82   "The whole world's future": Speech on June 5, 1947, announcing what became known as The Marshall Plan, available at https://www.marshallfoundation.org/the-marshall-plan/speech/.

82   It is "necessary to be bold": Thomas Paine, "Letter to Elihu Palmer," February 21, 1802, H.H. Clark, *Thomas Paine* (New York: American Book Company, 1944), 317.

82   "There is an amazing strength": Alexis de Tocqueville, *Democracy in America*, ed. Phillips Bradley (New York: Vintage, 1990), 1:247.

82   independent recodification commissions: These commissions could be modeled on the Base Realignment and Closing (BRAC) Commission structure, which used panels of independent experts to recommend base closings to Congress. In most iterations of the Commission, the Commission's recommendations were automatically approved unless Congress affirmatively rejected them by joint resolution, thus ensuring action except in the face of overwhelming political resistance. See, e.g., R. Chuck Mason, "Base Realignment and Closure (BRAC): Transfer and Disposal of Military Property," Congressional Research Service (February 28, 2013), 1.

83   That's more or less how new legal codes: Successful recodifications in history include the Justinian codes in the sixth century, the Napoleonic Code in the early nineteenth century, and the Uniform Commercial Code in the United States in the 1950s. In each case, the new code was proposed by a small committee of judges or legal scholars. See discussion and notes in Philip K. Howard, *The Rule of Nobody: Saving America from Dead Laws and Broken Government* (New York: W.W. Norton, 2014), 147–51.

83   pulverizes human spirit: "The evil of our times consists . . . in a kind of degradation, indeed in a pulverization, of the fundamental uniqueness of each human person." Karol Wojtyla (Pope John Paul II), letter to Henri du Lubac, as quoted in du Lubac, *At the Service of the Church* (San Francisco: Ignatius Press, 1993), 171–72.

83   "the supposed greater certainty": Friedrich A. Hayek, *Law, Legislation and Liberty*, vol. 1 (Chicago: University of Chicago Press, 1973), 116.

ACKNOWLEDGMENTS

Everyday Freedom came out of a paper I wrote for a conference on April 19, 2023, at Columbia on "Re-empowering Human Agency." The conference was sponsored by Common Good and Columbia's Center on Capitalism and Society, and covered by C-SPAN. The book draws on my prior writings, and includes substantial new material on human decision-making, on distrust and alienation, on the importance of institutions to personal freedom, and on the critical role of authority in a free society. Participants at the conference influenced my thinking and offered helpful feedback, including economists and Nobel laureates Edmund Phelps and Paul Romer, political scientist Jennifer Murtazashvili, historian Niall Ferguson, social philosopher Yuval Levin, public sector technology expert Jennifer Pahlka, management theorist Christian Madsbjerg, and public administration expert Paul Light. A participant at the conference, George Smith, provided helpful comments and suggested the title "everyday freedom."

Christopher DeMuth read early drafts, urging me on and suggesting new directions. Social psychologist Barry Schwartz was a close reader and corrected me in key places. Author Tim Carney gave valuable thematic feedback. Biographer Derek Leebaert made a key organizational suggestion. Adam White at The C. Boyden Gray Center suggested clarification of key points. Kent Walker at Google read several drafts with helpful reactions. Bob Whitcomb, long time editor at the *Providence Journal*, made many useful comments and line edits. My classmate and long-time adviser E. Donald Elliott suggested a number of valuable sources. Lord Leonard Hoffman introduced me to the thinking of Wesley Hohfeld. Sociologist Richard Arum provided helpful feedback. Ron Faucheux was there as a sounding board whenever I needed him. Professors Philip Bobbitt, Jonathan Haidt, and Travis Pantin pointed me in helpful directions. Mitch Daniels was encouraging. My friend David Patterson urged me to focus on questions of trust. Sean Brady was always thoughtful. My legal mentor John Warden gave reactions to a midstream draft. Stephen Pinto gave useful reader reactions.

The team at Common Good was indispensable, including Andy Park, Matt Brown, Ruth Mary Giverin, communications adviser Henry Miller, Seth Karecha, and Donna Thompson. Andy Park bore a disproportionate burden in helping produce this book, and his drive to get things right was extraordinarily valuable. Matt Brown is our legal sage, and reliably resourceful and wise. Henry Miller is my reality check, and Seth Karecha is a disciplined genius, including on matters of technology. Interns Roshan Pourghasemi, Will Sampson, and Charles Dutta found valuable material. Ruth Giverin makes the trains run on time, with a sense of humor. Donna Thompson quietly keeps us on the radar around the country. Blair Fitzgibbon, our DC communications adviser, is especially helpful in opening doors in the political world.

Arthur Klebanoff at Rodin Books and David Wilk at Booktrix leaned over backwards figuring out how to publish and distribute *Everyday Freedom*.

Common Good supporters and trustees were encouraging and generous, especially Scott Smith, Perry Golkin, Fritz Hobbs, John Messervey, Jim O'Shaughnessy, and Larry Mone. Bob Dilenschneider has already started opening doors.

Alexandra Cushing Howard kept telling me how important she thinks this book is, and put up with crazy hours and piles of books all over the house. I couldn't do much without her.

ABOUT THE AUTHOR

Philip K. Howard is a lawyer, author, and chair of Common Good (www.commongood.org), a nonpartisan organization aimed at replacing red tape with human responsibility. He grew up in Kentucky and lives in New York City.